DEMYSTIFYING INSURANCE

INSURANCE

A consumer's guide to Personal Property and Casualty Insurance

Dedicated to all my clients and insureds who have taken my council over the last thirty years, Thank you! Also thank you to www.irmi.com , International Risk Management institute who offers awesome information in the insurance business.

In addition, most of your policies are standardized, propagated and copyrighted by the ISO, Insurance Service Office. http://www.verisk.com/iso.html. In order to explain insurance coverage, we used some verbiage from many different companies using ISO policies.

Finally, because insurance is somewhat dynamic, my associates and I have set-up our website, demystifyinginsurance.com. Once registered, you can get updates on insurance, personal as well as commercial insurance as well as ask questions and request referrals for services.

To order additional copies please contact us at

http://demystifyinginsurance.com

DEMYSTIFYING INSURANCE

A consumer's guide to Personal Property and Casualty Insurance

2016

Christopher P. Kazor, CIC

DEMYSTIFYING INSURANCE

A consumer's guide to Personal Property and Casualty Insurance

2016

My disclaimer! The purpose of this book is to provide you information on how to read your policy and give you an idea of what is covered under standard personal lines policies and give you enough confidence to ask your agent questions! IN NO WAY AM I WARRANTING THAT YOUR POLICY WILL HAVE A CERTAIN COVERAGE. READ YOUR POLICY AND ASK QUESTIONS - CPK

The Basics

First of all, we are going to keep this very simple. In 1996, I penned a book *THE INSURANCE SURVIVAL HANDBOOK FOR THE NEW MILLENNIUM THE PRACTICAL WAY A FAMILY SHOULD PURCHASE INSURANCE.* That book droned on and on about every type of insurance and proved to be totally uninspiring and pointless.

This book will be remarkably different; we are going to talk about only Property and Casualty Insurance, which is Auto, Home, Dwelling / Landlord, and Excess Liability.

I am writing this as simply as possible and want the readers to get an idea of what to ask their agent and give the reader some translations of "insurance speak." We will talk about a coverage, explain how it works and why you should have it.

Now I know many of you are wondering who I am and what is my background, fair enough. My interest in risk started while I was working at Circus Circus Casino and attending summer school at UNLV, University of Nevada, Las Vegas. One compelling tidbit I picked up in the "Statistics of Casino Games Class" was casinos, and insurance companies essentially use the same equations to calculate the casinos "house percentage" or "insurance premium rate." No, we are not going to do permutations and combinations because you don't need to know that, but you need to understand that the insurance company is a giant casino, and you also need to remember that the house always wins.

After moving to Florida in the 70's, I worked at an independent insurance agency as a lowly customer service rep and quickly learned that it was the customer service representatives who knew about the policies, coverage and billing. It seemed that most of the agents were adept at public relations and golf, but it was the CSRs (customer service representatives) who ran the insurance agencies.

I was hired by K-Mart Insurance and sold insurance in K-Marts then became a "Direct Writer" for a national company owning my agency in Florida for eleven years. Hurricane Andrew in 1992 took a devastating toll on my agency and the company I represented. I was forced to sell the agency in 1996 and worked part time for an independent agency and taught Pre-license and Continuing Education classes for Florida. In 2006, I founded Nusurance ® an online insurance agency.

> ✓ *I mentioned that I was a Direct Writer, a Direct Writer is an agent who contracts with only one company and only that company. Examples would be State Farm Agents, Allstate Agents, and Nationwide Agents to name a few. These Agents must write for only that one company. An Independent Agent is an agent who represents many companies and has more flexibility to shop for you.*

One other thing I hope you will be able to do is to make smart insurance buying decisions for you and your family. When I make an insurance decision, I use a slot machine analogy the premium being the amount I put in the machine and the policy limit as the jackpot. We will explore that concept. We will also talk a lot about, purchasing coverage and getting the "most value" for your premium dollars.

Insurance BASICS

Like many Americans, you are paying a large part of your family's budget on insurance. I think buying insurance is extremely difficult. You are purchasing, an intangible, it is not like art you cannot display over your fireplace; it is not like a new car you cannot show it off; it is not even like buying a delicious meal you cannot enjoy it. Bottom line purchasing insurance is a bet. Yep, you heard me, it is a wager. The only difference in an insurance bet versus a casino bet is if you have won an insurance bet, you have lost. You have had some sort of loss.

The Two Types of Property and Casualty Insurance.

PROPERTY INSURANCE. Also known as First Party Insurance. If you have sustained a loss and the payment is made directly to "YOU" or someone has an interest like a lienholder or mortgage holder – the insurance is *PROPERTY INSURANCE*. If your laptop is stolen and you receive a check from the company - *PROPERTY INSURANCE*. If a tree has fallen on your car and you receive a check - *PROPERTY INSURANCE*. If you have a kitchen fire and the check from the insurance company is made out to BOTH you and your mortgage company that too is an example of *PROPERTY INSURANCE*.,

LIABILITY INSURANCE. I think the Brits have this right; they call liability insurance, "Third Party Coverage." With ***LIABILITY INSURANCE,*** we DO NOT pay you, but we will pay another (third party) you have injured because of your *negligence*. A TORT has been committed if you caused an accident with your auto and someone is injured, or you have damaged their property. A tort, in common law, is a civil wrong usually from a negligent act that has unfairly caused someone else to suffer loss or harm. If you are the one who committed the TORT, you are the **tortfeasor.** Please note that a tort is not necessarily an illegal act but causes harm, such a slander. Whether the tort is an illegal act or not, there are Liability coverages to protect you. Just a final note INTENTIONAL TORTS are EXCLUDED under all Liability policies.

Your Auto Insurance

Your auto is the second largest purchase you will make, and you must insure not only the auto but the damage that may be done by you or a permissive driver. So not only is it the second largest purchase it is your biggest liability exposure. So let's look at the components of a standard auto policy.

PART A – LIABILITY

- ✓ *Liability protects your assets in case you or permissive users of your auto are at fault in an accident. The other party can and most likely will file a lawsuit against you (the owner of the auto). At that time, your insurance carrier becomes your defense attorney (for a civil suit) to defend you and if the other party is successful pay up to the limits of liability you purchase.*
- ✓ *When you own an auto or other motor vehicle your assets, your home, your savings, your personal property and in some states even your future income by way of "Garnishment. "IS AT RISK ! Because a judgment rendered against you can be so devastating to you and your family, you must select and purchase adequate limits of "Liability Coverage."*

Each state has its minimum liability limits, but it is at this point that I will tell you my and our agency philosophy, that is retaining as much property exposure as you can and purchase as much liability coverage you can afford. In other words, take high deductibles on your property and purchase the most liability as you can afford.

Auto liability insurance is sold in "SPLIT LIMITS" or "CSL" (Combined Single Limit). "SPLIT LIMITS" essentially limits the company's exposure in an accident; it also is a negotiation tool for insurance adjusters. "SPLIT LIMITS" usually look like this 100/300/100. The first number is the maximum the company will cover you for the Bodily Injury (BI) for one person. The next number 300 is $300,000 the maximum that will be paid for all persons for Bodily Injury in an accident. The last number 100 is $100,000 for Property damage and ONLY property damage.

"CSL" (Combined Single Limit) is exactly that CSL 300 is $300,000, and that will be paid out without any sub-limits. The limits can be paid for BI or PD.

I know your next question. Which is best to purchase? Personally, I prefer Combined Single Limits but no matter what, the best thing is to consider an excess liability policy like an umbrella. Why? Listen carefully or get your highlighter.

✓ If there is a judgment found against you from an auto accident that is more than the coverage you have purchased, YOU ARE RESPONSIBLE TO PAY THE DIFFERENCE. If, however, the person suing you settles for policy limits. The company has gotten you off the hook. Again, Umbrella, Umbrella, Umbrella.

Here are some comparisons:

Split limits 100/300/100 vs. CSL 300

Scenario 1 You are at Fault

Person #1 injured $130,000

Person #2 injured $50,000

The other person's car was a Rolls Royce $140,000

Split limits 100/300/100

Person #1 injured $130,000 - $100,000 Paid by policy – you must pay $30,000

Person #2 injured $30,000 - $30,000 Paid by policy

The other person's car was a Rolls Royce $140,000 – Policy Pays $100,000 – you must pay $40,000

Total policy pay out $250,000 you must pay $70,000

CSL 300

Person #1 injured $130,000 - $130,000 Paid by the policy –

Person #2 injured $30,000 - $30,000 Paid by policy

The other person's car was a Rolls Royce $140,000 – Policy Pays $140,000 –

Total Policy Pay out $300,000 – You pay Zero

Split limits 100/300/100 vs. CSL 300

Scenario 2 You are at Fault

Person #1 injured $80,000 -

Person #2 injured $80,000

Person #3 injured $100,000

Person #4 injured $20,000

The other person's car was a totaled $55,000

With Split limits 100/300/100

Person #1 injured $80,000 - $80,000 Paid by Policy

Person #2 injured $80,000 - $80,000 Paid by Policy

Person #3 injured $100,000 - $100,000 Paid by Policy

Person #4 injured $20,000 - $20,000 Paid by Policy

The other person's car was a totaled $55,000-$55,000 paid for property damage

With Split limits - $280,000 BI total paid – and Property Damage of $55,000 paid – you pay nothing

With CSL limits 300

Person #1 injured $80,000 - $80,000 Paid by Policy

Person #2 injured $80,000 - $80,000 Paid by Policy

Person #3 injured $100,000 - $100,000 Paid by Policy

Person #4 injured $20,000 - $20,000 Paid by Policy

The other person's car was a totaled $55,000- ONLY $35,000 paid for property damage as the total limit is $300,000.

With CSL 300 - $280,000 BI total paid but only $35,000 for the property damage YOU pay $20,000.

Whether it is CSL or split limits I am always asked how much should I purchase, my answer is you should start with at least CSL of $300,000 or $500,000 plus an umbrella, but the client tells me, they do not want to be insurance poor, and they want low limits. If this is you, let me ask you a question. If you were in trouble and needed an attorney, what kind of lawyer do you want?   One with experience or someone new?

Of course, you want the best and most experienced attorney. Right?

Now I want you to be the head of litigation for YOUR insurance carrier. You have two files on your desk and two lawyers ready to be assigned cases. One lawyer is 50 years old has 30 years' experience and has won 85% of his cases. The other attorney is brand new, and this will be their first case.

The files, one has a limit of 10/20/10, and the other has limits of CSL $500,000. To whom will you assign each file? Your BEST and experienced lawyer will be assigned the higher limits. Some good news. Who pays for the lawyers? Your insurance company and the cost is OVER AND ABOVE the limit of liability you select.

Remember insurance is quite simple it is a wager, and you are purchasing bags of money or another way to think of it, you are playing different slot machines. If you pay the penny slots, your payout will be 10/20/10. If you play the dollar slots, the payout will be $500,000.

We live in a litigious society, and you must protect yourself. If you have an accident, you will be sued. If you are reading this and you are an athlete or personality you are a target. So if you are a weather person or a local celebrity in a small market; you need high limits and excess liability. If this is you, spend a few minutes reviewing your insurance policy and talking with your agent. Remember you are a target.

Part B Medical Payments

- ✓ Medical Payments under your auto insurance coverage pays expenses incurred for necessary medical and funeral services to persons injured by accident. These payments are without regard to fault or legal liabilities.

How medical payments are paid depends on whether or not you reside in a PIP state or not. For non-PIP states, medical payments is a convenience and will pay first dollar. In PIP state the medical payment coverage "subsidizes" the PIP coverage.

Coverage is per person per accident in increments of $500, $1,000, $2,000, $5,000 with some companies offering higher limits.

Most everyone will ask me if their health insurance will cover the injuries the answer is, maybe. I cannot answer that neither can your agent unless they read your health policy and with the advent of the

"Affordable Health Care Act" I truly do not know. Purchasing medical payments may be like wearing a belt with suspenders.

PART C Uninsured Motorist (UM)

- ✓ If you are NOT at fault in an auto accident, this coverage will pay for your damages should the at-fault driver have no coverage or not enough coverage to pay for your damages this coverage will pay for those damages.
- ✓ If you are covering the other guy with your liability shouldn't protect you and your family with at least the same coverage?

Uninsured motorist also underinsured motorist is a truly strange coverage. Uninsured motorist coverage applies only to Bodily Injury (BI), but many states do offer a property option.

Uninsured motorist comes into play when you are NOT AT FAULT in an accident, and you and passengers are injured, and the other party who IS AT FAULT has no insurance or low limits that will not cover the injuries.

Unfortunately, this coverage is most expensive in states that have the most uninsured drivers. According to Insurance Business America (http://www.ibamag.com) here are the top 10 uninsured states:

1. **Oklahoma:** 25.9%
2. **Florida:** 23.8%
3. **Mississippi:** 22.9%
4. **New Mexico:** 21.6%
5. **Michigan:** 21.0%
6. **Tennessee:** 20.1%
7. **Alabama:** 19.6%
8. **Rhode Island:** 17.0%
9. **Colorado:** 16.2%
10. **Washington:** 16.1%

The sad part the reasons for the uninsured motorist is political, and the cost of the UM coverage is driven up so much the insured must make the decision to cut some coverage and this important coverage is sometimes lowered or even dropped.

The limits are offered on a split limit or combined single limits. Generally, uninsured motorist claims do not go to court but are settled using arbitration.

Part D. Physical Damage – Damage to "YOUR AUTO"

✓ This coverage protects your auto and any non-owned auto damage.
✓ Your auto is the second largest purchase you will make this coverage will protect the auto itself.

Americans still have a love affair with their cars and some, unfortunately, care for their cars more than the other person or even their families well fair. Let me explain, one morning I had a gentleman come in our office that had just purchased a $63,000 auto.

His concern was for the physical damage to his car. When I presented a quote with liability, uninsured motorist medical payments and physical damage he was Incredulous that I would recommend a $5,000 deductible on a $63,000 vehicles. He wanted a $100 deductible.

He told me all he wanted to do was "Cover Damage to the Car."

I convinced him our agency was not for him and sent him down the street.

For most companies, there are two principal coverages they are "Collision" and "Other than Collision" AKA "Comprehensive."

Collision fairly simple – if you hit another auto or hit a stationary object or another auto hits you, the damage will be covered under the collision coverage. Damage to your auto is paid at the Actual Cash value to repair or replace your auto, less your deductible.

Other than Collision AKA Comprehensive covers anything that happens to your auto "Other than Collision" such as missiles, falling objects, fire, theft, larceny, explosion, earthquake, windstorm, hail, water, flood, vandalism, riot, civil commotion, contact with bird or animal, breakage of glass.

The question always comes up most is when should I drop my physical damage? It depends, we recommend high deductibles to save premium so if the ACV (Actual Cash Value) according to Kelly Blue Book ® or other references is $2,500 you should consider dropping your collision if you can afford a down payment on a new vehicle. If you are broke keep the coverage, the adjusters will help you get into some set of wheels.

However, Other than Collision" AKA "Comprehensive."(we are going to call it comp) Should never be dropped! First, the cost of coverage is minimal, but note Comp will cover glass breakage, and many states require the deductible be waived if a "windshield" needs to be repaired. The cost of replacing some of these van windshields can be as much as $1,800.

Another consideration is Comp will cover flood damage and one never knows if they are going to drive through 4 inches of water or 4 feet. KEEP YOUR COMP!

There are ancillary coverages under physical damage also first there is "Rental Reimbursement." This will give you a replacement vehicle if it is damaged either by a collision loss or a comp loss. Please note and understand the coverage will not respond should you just need a car for the maintenance.

I recommend our clients purchase this coverage if they only have one car or if both drivers work and one car would cause a hardship. Then the question is how much? You purchase this coverage in increments ranging from $20 per day with a $600 max up.

- ✓ If you are in an at-fault accident, you are subject to the rental reimbursement limit you purchase, However, if you are NOT AT FAULT in an accident, then if you drive a new Mercedes then the AT FAULT driver's insurance company MUST provide you with a replacement similar to your car.
- ✓ There are several other issues that have been decided on a state by state basis. One is aftermarket parts; some states allow insurance companies to use aftermarket parts other do not. The other issue is **Diminution in value.** Let's say you have just purchased a new BMW. While you are parked in your favorite coffee shop parking lot, some yeahoo jumps the curb and smashes into your brand new car. UGH. The fact is your one day old BMW will never be the same. Do you have a right to recover more than the ACV to repair?

To the writing of this book, the courts have ruled that if you are not at fault, the at-fault driver must **indemnify** you and pay the additional **Diminution in value.** Again as of this book, the courts have ruled that if you were at fault or there is an act of God covered by Comp, there is NO **Diminution in value payment required from the insured.**

The final coverage under physical damage is towing and labor. Although this seems to be inexpensive coverage we DO NOT recommend the coverage!

Of course, I will tell you why first I want you to remember our Slot Machine example. The towing and labor costs $3.95 per car per 6 months for a reimbursement of $50. So if, you only have one car $7.90 per year.

Would you play a slot machine where it would cost you $8 per pull, and the jackpot is only $50? No, you would not it is a lousy bet. We sell a private labeled towing service, but I understand many cell phone companies are offering car assistance.

I have one more reason not to purchase this coverage. If you purchase the towing and labor on your auto insurance policy and use it.

Wait for it!

It is counted as a claim. YEP, it is an incident and appears on your CLUE report.

Speaking of CLUE – How is your rate calculated

Ahh, you are now asking what CLUE is, it is CLUE (Comprehensive Loss Underwriting Exchange) this is a service which is generated by a company LexisNexis®, a consumer-reporting agency. The report contains up to seven years of personal auto and personal-property claims history. For those of you who do not know whom LexisNexis® is I recommend you Google® them, you see they know everything about you.

CLUE is used for underwriting all types of insurance, personal auto as well as homeowners, dwelling, and excess liability insurance. The CLUE report includes your name, Date of birth, policy number, date of loss, type of loss, the amount the company paid, description of the covered property, property address for homeowner claims or specific vehicle information for auto claims. The Companies report how much they paid out or if they even just set up a claim. The report will also report on claims that were denied.

The explanation of the CLUE report is an excellent segue into explaining how your insurance rate is calculated. To do this, I must, take you back to yesteryear, to the time when we calculated rates without computers. No way. Way!

Do you remember three ring binders? Each company would supply us with binders and 44,352 pages for every city in your state. You would customize the book for your city and perhaps a city near you, about 3,410 pages. Now you never tossed out the 40,942 in case someone from another county would come in for a quote.

Once you were customized your three ring binder quoting was relatively easy. Since you had the rates for your city, you would look up the liability section. Then, find the rate for the request limit and list it on your worksheet. You did it for each coverage, calculating the Comp and Collision was a bit more difficult as you have to go to the beige color (the vehicles were always the beige in all the companies) and find the make and exact model. You would enter those numbers on the worksheet. Then ask whom the youngest member of the household was. Then you would go to the yellow section and get a factor, If the youngest member if the house hold was an 18-year-old male the factor would be 2.8 X your rate. If the youngest person was 65, the factor was .6 x the factor and like magic you had the rate.,

There was a red section that added a premium for violations, but we ignored them since they were immensely complicated and no one ever had any violations anyway. In those days, the agent did not order the MVR (motor vehicle report) as it took weeks to get it from the state. Of course, if you were from Massachusetts you would never get it.

Today the computer does it all including applying what some think is a credit score but, in reality, is your "Insurance Score." To understand how this works, I want you to visualize a matrix with 500 boxes with five rows of 100 boxes, each row is a tier, and each box contains a factor or percentage. For illustration purposes, I am going to use .50 as the best factor which corresponds to the #1 Box the top left box #1. The factors increase .001 for each box so for our illustration box #500 will be 1.0.

Now, using every report known to man, you will be graded and like low golf score is best. Each company "Models" their insurance score, the score for one company may be a bit different than another depending on their underwriting appetite.

Here are some of the things that are included in your insurance score for many companies:

1. **Current insurance** – Generally the larger the company the better your score! No Prior is the kiss of death some companies will surcharge heavily.
2. **Time with current carrier** – If you have been with the company less than a year, your score will be graded adversely. Two to Three years you get a better score, three to five

better, and over 5 you usually are given the best score.

3. **Current Liability Limits** – Lower limits (10/20/10 (you should now know what that means)) are usually neutral. Credits are given for higher limits with generally the highest limits given for 100/300/100, with some companies giving higher limit outstanding credits.

4. **Marital status** - Married couples are considered more stable and given better credits than singles. Many companies will consider a widow or widower the same rare as a married couple.

5. **Age** – Most often 16 – 18 are the highest, 19 – 25 lower, 25 – 65 best rates. As we get older, however, companies are starting to sur charge us again, we never said any of this was fair.

6. **Sex** – Guys, the ladies are still better drivers than us but the gap is closing.

7. Credit Score – This is the touchy one, most insurance carriers believe that those with better credit have less claims.

8. **Home Ownership** – Home owners are given more credits than renters.

9. **Length of Time** at current address (owner or renter) The long you reside at your home, the more credit will be given.

10. **Occupation and Education** – Those who are engaged in a profession rather than a trade will get better credits and those who obtain college degrees also get better credits.

All of these credits are proprietary and companies keep them a secret. As I have been quoting coverage for over thirty years I have been able to recognize these rating factor, but not all companies are the same. Recently we were rating a medical doctor with a DUI. While one of our companies would not even give us a rate for him another weighted his occupation and education so much his rate was less than his prior carrier. One reason to use an independent agent who can shop many companies for you.

These scoring models and the weighting of each factor are dynamic and do change but those who score the lowest will be closer to the #1 Box on our matrix. Your driving record, zip code, and car type are still used to calculate the base rate just like we use to do with the three ring binder.

Confused?

Suffice it to say that unlike the days of yesteryear finding folks who have the same rate for the same car is rare. Last year I quoted auto insurance for identical twins. Both female, single, they owned condos next door to each other both had excellent credit. One was a teacher the other worked for a leading hotel chain and neither had a ticket or accident and yep, they purchased identical cars (different colors) and had a $100 difference in premium.

The companies are looking for stability, and responsibility and each company has its proprietary algorithm to calculate the rate. Remember a lapse in coverage is the kiss of death. If you have lapsed your insurance coverage for more than 30 days, you will pay as much as three times more than someone who has kept insurance in force for 36 months or more.

Insurance companies deem you responsible if you carry higher limits of liability own a home and have been at the same address for more than 36 months. Here is an issue. As the agent, I have no idea exactly how you were scored.

Remember LexisNexis®? They are the company who verifies all the insurance scoring factors. The only thing the insurance agent has access to is your MVR and maybe your CLUE report. But, do not ask for copies, agents must sign confidentiality agreements and although the agent can read you what is on your report if he or she copies and gives you a report, they are subject to a $10,000 fine and bamboo shoots under their fingernails.

Ask your agent to give you the phone number of the reporting company, call them, and they will either send you the report via email or snail mail. Yep, it is a copy of the same report. Go Figure!

DISCOUNTS !

Many of the things I have listed in the matrix are touted as "Discounts." Most states discounts have to be filed with the state regulators, and a definitive percentage is given off certain coverages. For example, you may get excited when you hear that if you have an anti- theft device like a car recovery system you will get a 10% discount.

WOW! 10% - You think $1,000 per 6 months for your policy 10% will be $200 per year, GREAT! Well not so, the 10% is applied only to the coverage to which theft applies, OTC -Other than Collision also known as Comprehensive Coverage. Of the $1000 per 6 months, only $57 applies for OTC so now 10% of $57 is $5.70 or $11.40 per year not as good as the $200 per year, but it is lunch.

GOOD DRIVER / CLAIM FREE DISCOUNT
Every company has some bonus for having not tickets or accidents in the last 36 months. Some companies may even reward you with more of a discount if your record is clear for 60 months. These **GOOD DRIVER / CLAIM FREE DISCOUNT** can be significant maybe as much as 20%.

Here, I need to point out a fact every driver needs to know that is the understanding the evil "surcharge." Companies will add a premium to those folks who have a ticket or accident, even "NOT AT FAULT" accidents. Each company has its schedule but, having a major speed, usually over 15 miles an hour over the speed limit or an at-fault accident can increase your premium 15% to 20%.

Now, for some shocking news. I get calls every day from insureds who have been with a certain company for several years and has just had an accident if this is you be prepared to get majorly DOUBLED ZAPPED. Remember your **GOOD DRIVER / CLAIM FREE DISCOUNT** and I said they can be a significant discount, well it is GONE! Not only is it gone, you most likely will be surcharged for the infraction. But, you say "I have "Accident Forgiveness" you do but depending on the company you will not be surcharged, but you will most likely lose your **GOOD DRIVER / CLAIM FREE DISCOUNT.**

I know, you are upset about the "NOT AT FAULT" accident. Well, about eight years ago companies started to count **"INCIDENTS"** an incident is anything that was reported to the company even lockouts and towing services. There are some states who are extremely consumer friendly who bar companies for charging anything for, not at fault incidents some not. There are many states who are

"Comparative Negligence" states. Here, each accident is negotiated between claims adjusters and even if you were not ticketed for the accident the claims adjuster to close the file attributed a percentage that you were at fault. Save your breath except for appealing to your state legislator there is not much you can do. Change companies, this may be the worst thing you can do especially if you have had tenure with the incumbent carrier.

RETIRED DISCOUNTS Hey finally you get something getting old. A special note, in a few PIP, states the retired discount is tied to the REMOVAL of WORK LOSS BENEFITS. Years ago I insured a gentleman who insisted on his RETIRED DISCOUNT. He was hurt in a car accident but claimed work loss as he was a full-time manager at a convenience store. The claim was denied. PLEASE NOTE if you are working DO NOT request the discount.

AFFINITY DISCOUNTS When shopping for new auto insurance do not overlook associations you belong to. I know that if you belong to a certain college alumni associations you get bombarded by several insurance companies offering discount, professional organizations in some states will also have a nexus to an insurance carrier.

MILITARY DISCOUNTS - Thank you for serving! There are companies who work only with military folks. USAA for one and I must say their customer service always ranked number one in surveys. After reading many of their policies offered to me by insureds, I must tell you the writing of their policies favor their insureds / members more than any other company I am familiar with. If you are current Military or retired, it may be worth a call to check your eligibility. Other companies do offer military discounts, but it is only for active military, and the discount is only on medical payments that apply to related medical coverages.

MULTI-POLICY DISCOUNTS Many companies offer "Package" or Multi-Policy Discounts. Always ask.

LOW MILEAGE DISCOUNT. This use to be a substantial discount but too many agents wanting a competitive edge would give the discount to everyone which in the long run "eroded the discount" and today you will find that this discount is less than 1%. But, ASK YOUR AGENT if the company offers a **LOW MILEAGE DISCOUNT.** You will find the discount applies for those who drive less than 7,500 per year. I see this discount making a comeback where some companies will use mechanical devices to gauge your driving.

Speaking of mechanical devices, Progressive Insurance is doing an excellent job with their "Snap Shot®" device. Nearly 80% of our clients who have tried the device has had enormous success with one of our clients saving 45%. Older cars may not be eligible as you will have to plug it into a service port, After 30, days it evaluates your driving, and if eligible will apply discounts. If your independent agent represents Progressive ® a call to your agent may be worth it. Progressive has rolled out the Snap Shot quickly, but other companies are seeing the benefit and starting their programs. Look for more of these type discounts to come.

HOMEOWNER DISCOUNT Remember to tell your agent you own a home, condo or Mobile home you may benefit twice, once on your insurance score but also many companies offer "another" discount. Note, if your home is in the name of a "living trust" the company may ask for proof that you are the beneficiary of the trust.

When securing the best rate from an agent "ALWAYS" have the VIN Vehicle Identification Number and give it to the agent., Without the **VIN** you are not getting a quote but a "Rate Guess" since today there are so many models and each model has different equipment including safety devices. Here is a list of discounts that will be applied if your car has

these safety devices even if you do not know you
have them.

ANTI LOCK BREAK DISCOUNT – applied to all
coverages except Uninsured Motorist.

AIR BAGS -Your **VIN** will tell the agents rating
computers how many airbags you have and give you
the proper discount. This discount will be applied to
Medical Payments coverage, Uninsured Motorist and
if you live in a PIP state PIP. This discount will only
apply to coverages that have to do with Bodily Injury
to you and your passengers.

ANTI-THEFT   you may know you have some Anti-
Theft device, but only the **VIN** will reveal the exact
type.

Companies also will give discounts for Crash
Resistant Doors, Electronic Stability Systems (EBS)
and even Daytime Running Lights you may not even
know you have these features but your **VIN** will.

Lastly, I want to talk about two relatively new
discounts, the "FULL PAY" discount and the
"PAPERLESS" discount. The **"PAID IN FULL"/"**
FULL PAY" discounts have become an immensely
powerful discount. I recently insured a client where
the full pay option was over a 20% discount. Also if,
possible look for a company that will offer a year
policy term. The advantage is you will be locked into

the rate for one year, and many of the companies will give you the "**PAID IN FULL**"/" **FULL PAY**" discount with two six month payments. If you do the math, this is a significant discount.,

The last discount needs to be discussed. The **"PAPERLESS"** and also know known as the **"GREEN DISCOUNT"** can be as much as 5% of the total premium although this may seem to be exciting it is not for everyone.

Our agency profiles our clients before we offer this discount. If you are an email freak and are one of those folks who check their email every hour, or who has your email sent to your phone AND THE ABILITY to print from the phone of another device, then this discount may be for you! However, if you are a casual email user or a person who cannot remember how to access the account DO NOT even think of taking advantage of this discount.

Many times the company, not your agent will send you an offer to save money by "signing up" online. Of course, you like 95% of all consumers will not read the terms. In return for the discount, you will not receive ANY further communications by mail, including but not limited to Renewal and Cancelation notices.

Moral of the story if you want to receive mail do not take advantage of the discount!

So let's play the Auto Insurance Slot Machine!

A couple things you need to know, we are going to keep this simple and not use complete **Combinations and permutations, just some simple math, our assumptions and percentages were simply found via a google search** . Next , Probability vs. Odds. Probability is the likely hood of an event happening. Could be a roll of the dice, a car accident, your home being destroyed by fire. Odds is the "Ratio" between the wagered and the payoff. House percentage is the relationship of the odds and the probability to determine a fraction. If the fraction is more than one, the advantage is to the house, if less than one advantage player.

The Auto Liability Slot Machine.

Your Wager is average cost of auto liability insurance in the US is between $1000 and $1,400 (ehow.com) a year for $100,000 / $300,000 / $100,000 – Should you be "AT FAULT" in a catastrophic accident the maximum pay out would be $400,000, $300,000 Max BI Liability and $100,000 in PD Liability. Now let's use that probability of being AT FAULT in a catastrophic accident in your life times is .00357.

The Max Payout (Jackpot) is $400,000 times .00357 = $1,428 a year. Say you are paying $1,400 (Wager) the house percentage is .98 under 1 percent. An estimated profit of 2% of the premium.

If you decide to by the lowest limit $10,000 / $20,000 / $10,000 where that maximum pay out by the company will be $30,000. But you can save 40% on your premium paying $857 a year, now let's look at the house percentage. So now the cost of playing this slot machine is $857 with a $30,000 Jackpot.

Max Payout is $30,000 Times .00357 = $107.10. So $107/ $857 / the odds with a house percentage of .87% or an estimated profit of 13% profit or return to the insurance company.

One of the reasons insurance companies can run a house percentage just under 100% for those who purchase high limit is so many folks decide to purchase lower coverages, thus subsidizing those who carry high limits.

If you have the time and the desire you can set up a simple calculation for every policy and every coverage. The problem is gathering the relevant statistics. Insurance companies are very secretive about their losses and the causes thereof. So many time you rely on a "Google®" search). If you do this you will find that some coverages, like collision, are a bad bet and you should self-insure. But this is where human nature kicks in, I just got this bright and shiny new car, I do not want to pay for it again; so you buy the coverage.

Insuring your Home –
Home Owners – Renters – and Condo Insurance

✓ The broad term "Homeowners" is used for Homeowner, Condo Owners (also Co-ops) and even apartment dweller. These policies are "Package" policies which provide you with a bundle of coverages including Liability as well as Property.

Remember; we are going to keep this book as simple as possible. I caution everyone to READ THEIR POLICY and counsel with their insurance agent. All insurance policies are not written the same. The policies we are going to discuss are standard ISO (Insurance Service Office) policies, and your policy may be different. If you are reading this in Florida or Louisiana; they are very different. We are going to discuss three policies, the Standard Homeowners Policy the HO3, the Condominium Policy HO6 and the Renters Policy HO4. To be eligible for the HO3 you must be the owner AND MUST LIVE in a one - four family dwelling., A HO6 must be an owner of the Condominium unit insured but may either live in it or rent it out to another. The HO4 is known as the

"Renters" policy and is for the renter of any livable unit.

Homeowners insurance is less confusing than auto insurance. The name of this book is Demystifying Insurance, and that is what we want to do. Home Owners Insurance is a package policy as it has both components of Property coverage as well as Liability combined in one policy. First, we will talk about the property coverage of the policy. The property policy consists of two lists. One list is "Stuff we are going to cover." The second list is a list of perils or a list of "Things that can happen to my stuff". If something from the list of covered stuff is damaged by a peril on the list of things that can happen to my stuff, the company will pay the claim, subject to a deductible.

Section I Standard Homeowners policy - Property
The Property section of a standard Homeowners Policy defines what is covered. Under the Homeowners, we define what is covered by defining coverages:

Coverage: A – The Dwelling itself. The Building and *"all structures attached."* Those of you living in what I call CAT States, Catastrophic State, Florida, Louisiana and South Carolina. PLEASE REVIEW your policy. In Florida some policies have modified the "A" Coverage to "EXCLUDE" anything under the original roof line. Again, never assume all policies are the same.

Anything attached to the home, patios, decks, fences screened porches, will be considered part of Coverage A.

Coverage B - Other Structures" covers private structures on the residence premises that are not attached to the main dwelling, such as a detached garage, guest house, fence, tennis court or storage building.

Coverage C – Personal Property or as I call it Your Stuff. Imagine your home was a doll house. Then pretend to take off the roof, any of your stuff that falls out is Personal Property and is covered under Coverage C. Anything that is "Glued and or Screwed" and does not fall out is covered under Coverage A The Dwelling.

Your Stuff is covered World Wide, but with a couple of exceptions, one is if you have an additional residence your stuff will be covered at the second location but only to 10% of your "C Coverage" listed on your **DECLARATIONS PAGE or DEC PAGE.**

> ✓ *Information -- your*
> *DECLARATIONS PAGE or DEC*
> *PAGE is the first page of any*
> *insurance policy, it lists the kind of*
> *insurance, your name, address,*

***insured address and limits of
coverage.***

The second limitation is a new one and is just now
being adopted, and that is your stuff in a storage unit.
Before 2010, there was no limitation on your personal
property in storage, however, now whatever you have
in storage is limited to 10% of your "C Coverage"
listed on your **DECLARATIONS PAGE or DEC
PAGE.**

Now do not assume that all your stuff is covered or
covered without limitations. I need to refer you to
your policy. Get it; I will wait. Ok now that you are
back, go ahead and find the property section of your
policy. I am going to summarize it, but the dollar
amounts may be different depending on the state of
the company.

STUFF EXCLUDED:

Now remember we are talking about "PROPERTY
INSURANCE" remember direct payment to you?
First Specifically insured articles are excluded. Of
course, I will explain, let's say you have a ring which
you insure under a "PERSONAL ARTICLES
FLOATER" as it is insured under a specific policy it
is specifically excluded for payment under your
"Coverage C" Remember no double dipping.

Animals, birds or fish, are excluded, again we are
talking about, property coverage, payments to you. In
1989, one of my insureds had a kitchen fire, there was

about $12,000 of damage to the kitchen, but his Toucan Bird died of smoke inhalation. Set aside the emotional cost the replacement cost of the rare bird was $3,800, The Bird WAS NOT COVERED.

Motorized vehicles such as riding lawn mowers, and other types of vehicles that service an insured's residence and ANY device to assist the handicapped are covered but your $2,500 ATV is not covered.

What about my Portable Sirus Radio. UGH may be covered or may not be covered, sorry you did not want to hear that. OK for "Portable electronic equipment" that reproduces, receives or transmits audio, visual, or data signals and is designed to be operated ONLY by the power from the electronic system of a motorized vehicle. However, if it is out of the car at the time of loss and it can operate on BOTH the car and another external power source, then it will be covered subject to your deductible.

You thought that explanation was complicated, let's talk about your son's hobby Aircraft, and its parts are covered but only for certain perils which we will talk about later. However real Aircraft and Aircraft Parts are excluded.

2016 Update and a new conundrum.

Before December 21, 2015, I would have told you that your "Hobby Craft Drone" would be covered under your homeowners policy for both physical damage (for certain named perils) and liability. But now I contend there is no coverage.

Effective December 21, 2015, anyone who owns a small unmanned aircraft of a certain weight must register with the Federal Aviation Administration's Unmanned Aircraft System (UAS) registry before they fly outdoors. People who do not register could face civil and criminal penalties.

In essence, when you register your drone, you have acknowledged it is an *AIRCRAFT,* and I predict the insurance companies will deny any losses sustained by their use. A separate Drone or UAV insurance coverage will become mandatory.

Those of you who own your personal Hovercraft do not assume that it is covered under your homeowners policy because it IS NOT and neither are its replacement parts. Also, there is no coverage.

There is NO COVERAGE for Property of roomers, boarders or other tenants unless such persons are related to you. Property in an apartment that is regularly rented or available for rental to others and property that is rented or held for rental to others away from the residence premises is excluded; however, some policy will allow $2,500 for "landlord furnishings" on the residence premises.

Working from home? We are going to have a section on that, but you must understand that the business data, "YOUR INPUT" whether contained in books and paper records or electronics software media is NOT COVERED. Now there is coverage for the cost of blank records or media and of prerecorded retail computer programs is covered subject to the property used in business limitation, we will discuss that soon.

The last EXCLUSION we are going to talk about is water or steam. WATER? Yep, water. Say you go on vacation, and while you were gone a pipe broke. When you return from vacation and open your door, 22,000 gallons of water comes out. Well, the damage done by the water IS COVERED! But, when you get your water bill for $6,000 for 22,000 gallons of water there will be no help from your homeowners policy.

You must be aware of, not only is some of your stuff excluded there are limitations.

LIMITATIONS ON YOUR STUFF

We already talked about the Coverage C limit for Storage facilities and secondary premises remember, it is 10% of the Coverage C Limit listed on your DEC page. But there is a lot more if you keep a lot of cash on hand, the maximum amount you will pay should there be a loss is only $200 per occurrence for the loss of money or related property, platinum other than platinum ware, gold other than goldware, silver other than silverware, stored value cards, and smart cards.

$1,500 per occurrence applies to securities, and similar property, $1,500 per occurrence applies to watercraft, including their trailers, accessories and equipment and trailers, not used, with watercraft subject to covered causes of loss

The next limitations are extremely confusing the limit is $1,500 per occurrence applies to loss by **THEFT** of jewelry, watches, furs, precious and semi-precious stones. $2,500 per occurrence applies to loss by **THEFT** of silverware, goldware, and pewter ware. $2,500 per occurrence applies to loss by **THEFT** of firearms and related equipment. Please notice the limitation only applies to **THEFT!** So should there be a fire and you have $5,000 or jewelry, $10,000 in silverware and $15,000 in guns the policy will pay $30,000 less your deductible, why because the cause of the loss was FIRE!

I promise I will discuss insuring doing business from your home, but you need to understand this limitation. First, loss "ON PREMISES" the maximum you have for a covered loss of **"BUSINESS PERSONAL PROPERTY"** is $2,500. (unendorsed) So if you have a business where you keep $5,000 of inventory in your garage, and there is a pipe break what is the maximum you will get? $2,500! What if you have a home break in. Your $4,000 laptop that you use in **BUSINESS** and your two other computers one $3,000 your wife used, and another $3,000 used by your children is stolen. The policy (ignoring deductible) will pay $8,500 - $6,000 for your wife's and children's computers and a maximum of $2,500 for your computer because it is **USED IN BUSINESS.**

For **"BUSINESS PERSONAL PROPERTY" off-premise,** we have now classified the property as electronic and non-electric. Say you are an artist and have a $2,000 Leather Portfolio, and it is stolen from your car at your favorite coffee shop. The MAXIMUM we will pay is $500.

If, however, you had a $2,000 laptop stolen, the maximum we will pay is $1,500. Further, this "electronic apparatus" limitation applies to portable electronic equipment (cellular phones, stereos, computers. Bottom line you have $1,500 in laptop coverage whether or not it is used in business or not.

> ✓ *Before we discuss the next coverage I want to introduce you to new terms, they are DIRECT LOSS and INDIRECT LOSS. So far we have talked about coverages A B C, and any loss to those coverages would be a DIRECT LOSS. Any "tangible loss to the property will be considered a DIRECT LOSS. Let's say you have a house fire, and you sustain a DIRECT LOSS to the Dwelling (Coverage A) your detached garage (Coverage B) was also destroyed and, of course, all of your stuff, personal property (Coverage C) was also destroyed. But, you still have another loss. Where are you going to live or if you have a duplex where are you getting to get your rent? Many folks*

*do not realize that even after a loss, you are responsible for the mortgage! So with that in mind, I will introduce our next coverage that will cover your **INDIRECT LOSS,** that is a loss of cash flow from your rent or cash you must pay out to live.*

Coverage D – Under the standard homeowners policy, *"Loss of Use" or ADDITIONAL LIVING EXPENSES (ALE),* covers increases over normal living costs if damage from a covered peril makes the residence unfit for occupancy.If it is duplex, triplex or quad it will also pay for the *"Fair Rental Value"* if the rental units are also unfit for occupancy.

OK, Now that we have defined what is covered I know you want to know how much coverage you get. In most state the company by the use of replacement cost estimator software sets the replacement cost of your dwelling, that is Coverage A. Let's use $300,000

Then under standard HO3 contract, you will have 10% of Coverage A or $30,000 for Coverage B, Detached structures. Your Coverage C is 50% of the A coverage or $150,000. Finally, your Coverage D, Additional Living Expense (ALE) is 30% of Coverage A or $30,000.

Remember I said property insurance is two lists, one is things we will cover and the other a list of things that can happen to your stuff called perils. Those are "Causes of Loss."

For the standard HO3, there are TWO lists; one is for Coverage A, B, D and another for Coverage C, your stuff. OK, let's start with Coverage A, B, D we apply "OPEN PERILS" or ALL RISK EXCEPT WHAT IS EXCLUDED. What?

If the dwelling itself is damaged, we (the insurance company) will pay if anything happens to your home as long as it is not EXCLUDED., Still have your policy? Look for Section 1 exclusions for Coverage A. There are several exclusions, Ordinance or Law which can be "Bought Back" by purchasing an endorsement, (Some State Require 10% of Coverage A)

Ordinance or Law is an Ordinance or Law requiring or regulating the construction, demolition, remodeling, renovation or repair of property, including removal of any resulting debris. For example, if your home was built with non-hurricane windows and after a fire the local ordinance requires hurricane windows the insurance company will be obligated only to replace non-hurricane windows, and you will be required to pay the difference between the non-hurricane windows and the better windows. You may purchase an endorsement.

> ✓ *If you have a new home, you may not need Ordinance or Law Coverage. As your home gets older, we recommend adding at least 10% of Ordinance or Law endorsement.*

Other Exclusions: theft from a dwelling under construction, wear, and tear, rust, damage from insects, vermin mold, rot, smog, industrial smoke, and settling just to name a few, some other general exclusions are water damage from flood, rising waters, backing up of sewers or drains, underground seepage; power failure that occurs **away** from the residence; neglect to use reasonable means to save and preserve property at and after a loss; war; nuclear hazards; intentional loss created by or at the direction of an insured; and governmental action. Consult your policy. Now if what happened to you home is NOT listed in EXCLUSIONS, it is covered.
For your Coverage C, your stuff, it is a bit easier, but the coverage is much less broad. The "Broad Form Covered Cause of Loss" applies. This is a "Named Peril form which covers loss by:

Fire; lightning; windstorm; hail; explosion; riot or civil commotion; aircraft; vehicles; smoke; vandalism or malicious mischief; theft; falling objects; weight of ice, snow or sleet; accidental discharge or overflow of water or steam from within a plumbing, heating, air conditioning or sprinkler system or household appliance; sudden and accidental tearing apart, cracking, burning or bulging of a steam or hot water heating, air conditioning or sprinkler system or water heating appliance; freezing of a plumbing, heating, air conditioning, sprinkler system or household appliance; sudden and accidental damage from artificially generated electrical current; volcanic eruption and if your "Stuff Coverage" as defined is damaged by the above perils, the policy will respond.

The HO6 – The Condo Policy:

If you are a Condo Dweller, and you are not sure what the Condo Association will cover in case of loss, DO NOT ASK, Bob, your neighbor. Read your condo's current docs and then if it is not clear call the property manager. Unless the state you reside in has a Statute guiding what is and is not covered by the Condo's master property policy, the Condo Docs will be the ruling document.,

If you live or own a condo in Florida FL718 makes it easy for us, the unit owner is responsible for all personal property within the unit or limited common elements, and floor, wall, and ceiling coverings, electrical fixtures, appliances, water heaters, water filters, built-in cabinets and countertops, and window treatments, including curtains, drapes, blinds, hardware, and similar window treatment components, or replacements of any of the foregoing which are located within the boundaries of the unit and serve only such unit. Such property and any insurance thereupon is the responsibility of the unit owner.

You must know what is covered to establish your Coverage A, in most states, for the condo (Coverage A) it includes improvement and betterments and everything that is "Screwed and Glued" to it including your refrigerator. If you have made extensive improvement Condo Docs will only replace the Condo unit to the "Kind and Quality" that the developer originally installed, and you will be responsible for the difference.

There is no Coverage B under the condo policies. However, if you are responsible for a Detached Car Port, please council with your agent to cover it properly.

Your Coverage C is probably easy for you to calculate again it is your stuff, clothes, shoes, furniture, kid's toys, games, linens, pillows. You select the best number.

On Standard Condo Policies your Coverage D (ALE) is 50% of your Coverage C, so If you select $50,000 of Coverage C, you have $25,000 in Coverage D, Additional Living Expense.

Special note! Unendorsed the "Broad Form Named Peril" cause of loss form applies, you must make sure your agent endorsed the Coverage to "Open Perils". Here is the significance of this. Unendorsed if you accidentally drop a heavy object on your ceramic tile, and it breaks you will have NO COVERAGE! Why? Accidentally dropping an object is not named on the list. Another example is if you have a kitchen counter and you "scorch it" with a hot pot. Unendorsed again there will be NO COVERAGE for the damage. If you would have had your agent endorse your policy with "Open Perils" (Also known as Special Form" both of our examples would have been covered.)

The HO4, the RENTERS POLICY.

It seems every week, we hear of an apartment fire, and we are told that the residents of said apartment are displaced, and those folks are being taken in at the Red Cross facility some other social service and have lost everything. A renter's policy if anything is inexpensive and is an excellent value for the price.

The Renters policy essentially has Coverage C, personal property which you will select. Your Coverage D is 30% of your Coverage C, so if you select $50,000 in your Coverage C, you will have $15,000 for ALE (Additional Living Expenses), so when there is a fire, you will have $15,000 to get yourself in a hotel rather than sleeping on a cot somewhere. And the next day you can get with a claims adjuster and arrange for $50,000 of new stuff. Truly a bargain.

Your Coverage C under the Renters policy is "Broad Form Named Peril" only a few companies will endorse your Coverage C to "Open Peril" or "Special Form."

ADDITIONAL COVERAGE

Under the standard Homeowners policy "Additional Coverages" are granted. After a loss, you are responsible for cleaning up the mess the good news is you have the Cost of debris removal and reasonable repairs after a loss are covered up to 5% of the Coverage A limit as "ADDITIONAL INSURANCE.

SPECIAL NOTE! – Additional Coverages are good but are granted within the policy limit, however, if the grant of coverage is ADDITIONAL INSURANCE", then the coverage will be paid OVER the limit. Example, if your Coverage A is $300,000 and is a Total loss, you will have $15,000 OVER the $300,000 to pay for Debris Removal.

Trees, shrubs and plants are covered up to 5% of the Coverage A limit ADDITIONAL INSURANCE, but not more than $500 for any one tree, shrub or plant, and only for certain limited perils of Fire, Lightning, Explosion, Riot, Civil Commotion, Aircraft,

Vandalism Malicious Mischief (VMM) or vehicle, not owned by the insured or resident of the premises. Note, windstorm IS NOT A PERIL for trees.

What the Policy will pay is up to $500 reimbursement is provided for fire department service charges.
ADDITIONAL INSURANCE

Thirty days coverage is allowed for property removed from endangered premises, for loss from ANY cause. NOT ADDITIONAL INSURANCE. Note we said ANY loss, in 1993 one of our clients was told to evacuate from a barrier island. On the way out of town, their van was swept up by flooding waters and the van and all their personal property was lost. Now remember FLOOD IS EXCLUDED under the Homeowners Policy, but since they were evacuating and the loss occurred because they were evacuating we paid the claim, again for a loss from ANY cause.

The policy will pay loss from unauthorized use of credit cards or fund transfer cards, forgery, and acceptance of counterfeit money is covered up to $500. NOT ADDITIONAL INSURANCE.

The Policy will pay, Coverage of $1,000 applies for loss assessments imposed by an association against the insured for damage to property caused by a peril insured against under Coverage A. Let me explain, first of all, you must be a member of a homeowner association or condo association. If common property is damaged and for one reason there is not adequate insurance held by the association the association will "ASSESS" all the members of the association. If the loss to the association property, would have been, a covered peril under the homeowner's policy, the policy will afford up to $1,000 for the loss.

Here is an example, there is a lightning strike on the association rec room, the insurance covered $100,000 of a $150,000 loss. If there are 100 homeowners each member will be assessed $500. 500 x 100 = 50,000. The homeowner can submit the assessment to the insurance carrier, and it will be paid without a deductible.

We mentioned that there was no Coverage A under the Renters Policy, although this is true there is 10% of Coverage C is available, as an additional amount of insurance, for building additions and alterations made or acquired at the tenant's expense. So if you have $50,000 of Coverage C, Personal Property and if you installed a $5,000 bookcase and it is destroyed by a covered loss you will have the $5,000 to replace the bookcase.

SPECIAL NOT TO FLORIDA AND CAT STATES, ADDITIONAL LIVING EXPENSES ARE NOT ISO % AND ARE DIFFERENT COMPANY TO COMPANY.

Other Property Issues:

Settling a Loss.

Replacement Cost Valuation (RCV) vs. Actual Cash Value (ACV)

Before we get into the concepts of Replacement Cost Valuation (RCV) vs. Actual Cash Value (ACV) I need to explain an extremely fundamental concept of insurance and the is the "Principal of Indemnity" That is to make one whole again. All basis of all insurance policies is to put the insured in the "Same Financial Position" as they were before the loss occurred.

The **basic** property insurance policies will respond and will pay the **ACTUAL CASH VALUE (ACV)** of the property at the time of the loss, but not more than the amount required to repair or replace. The loss is always subject to the dollar policy limit stated on the **DEC PAGE** of the policy. Courts have rules that ACV, it is the current costs to repair or replace the item, *less an allowance for depreciation.*

I see some of you are a bit confused by my above statement. Please remember I said the BASIC Property policy that would be any one that is not endorsed or modified.

REPLACEMENT COST VALUE (RCV) is an ACCEPTED deviation to the concept of indemnity. Pure indemnity would be the settlement of paying **ACTUAL CASH VALUE.** Although the payment of ACV is **PURE INDEMNITY,** it was not a popular settlement. Many policies modified their policies, so the more popular **REPLACEMENT COST VALUE** was written into, the more deluxe policies or was offered as an option.

In the standard Homeowner, "Coverage A" is paid on **REPLACEMENT COST VALUE** (RCV) as long as the policy limit is, *AT THE TIME OF LOSS,* is equal to 80% or more of the replacement cost. *AT THE TIME OF LOSS?* Correct. One of the first things an adjuster will do is to order the property tax records and using software establishes the replacement cost of your home.

 If the policy limit of your home is within 80% of the adjusters calculation, at the time of loss, the adjuster will authorize replacement of your property up to the Coverage A limit as shown on your **DEC PAGE.**

IMPORTANT

 I cannot stress enough to make sure your home is properly valued as if the replacement is not within 80% the company then will pay the **ACTUAL CASH VALUE** (ACV) or a proportional amount based on coinsurance, whichever is to the least detriment to the insured.

1. Your home is insured for $400,000 – the value at the time of loss is $500,000. Your home will be replaced up to $400,000.
2. Your home is insured for $400,000 – the value at the time of loss is $600,000. Your home will NOT be replaced. It will be paid the greater of the **ACTUAL CASH VALUE (ACV)** or $400,000/(600,000 x .80) or 83% of the loss.

REPLACEMENT COST VALUE (RCV) for your Coverage C, your stuff is different you must make sure to request the agent "endorse **REPLACEMENT COST VALUE** (RCV) for your stuff. In some states, many companies automatically add the endorsement, but you must ask the agent if they include **REPLACEMENT COST** on your personal property, your Coverage C. When you are shopping for replacement homeowners, ask to review the quote and make sure that **REPLACEMENT COST VALUE** is endorsed.

Deductibles

In CAT states*, the wind or windstorm deductibles are separated and usually expressed in percentages.

For example, 2% Wind and $1000 AOP. AOP? ALL OTHER PERILS, other than wind.

*the CAT States, are States that are prone to Catastrophic losses from Hurricanes.

✓ Although it may seem simple, you must remember that the deductible is subtracted from the loss NOT THE LIMIT. Here are a couple of limits. You insure your home for $500,000, the replacement cost at a loss was $525,000, and you have a $5,000 deductible.

First, you are within 80% of replacement so you will receive the replacement up to $500,000 the limit of the policy. But, you have a $5,000 deductible. Don't worry, remember you take the deductible $5,000 from the loss. The loss is $525,000 - $5,000 = $520,000 but to the policy limit shown on the DEC PAGE which is $500,000.

Section II - Standard Homeowners Policy - Liability

Of course, covering your property is essential, but the liability insurance covers your assets including your home. In Florida because of the $75 BILLION of property losses due to hurricanes homeowner insurance rates are the highest in the US many consumers of means have decided "Self-Insure" their homes. From a risk management standpoint, it is hard to disagree about the property coverage but NEVER go without liability coverage.

One of my clients an elderly man widowed and had assets informed me he was not going to purchase coverage that year because of the prohibited price. I understood but his reasoning but offered him a liability only policy.

He said, "Mr. Kazor, I have lived in that home for 35 years, and no one has ever tripped and neither fell nor have I ever did anything to get sued."

My response simple. "A European roulette wheel has the numbers 1-36, plus a slot for zero."

My insured nodded, smiled and wrote the check for the liability policy as he said, "Just in case I hit Zero."

Under Section II-Liability, there are two Coverages, Coverage E – Liability and Coverage F – Medical Payments also known as "Guest" Medical Payments. Let's discuss Coverage F first. I like using **GUEST MEDICAL PAYMENTS** describes the coverage better. The term " GUEST " tells you that there will be no benefit for anyone living in the home. I tell my clients it is "GOOD GUY COVERAGE." Should someone get hurt on your property, you have a bag of money, the coverage is known as **GUEST MEDICAL PAYMENTS** to patch them up *without admitting liability.* This coverage comes in handy at your child's birthday party when your neighbors fall and chips a tooth.

Coverage E Liability Coverage is "Comprehensive Personal Liability "will cover your personal, **_nonbusiness_** activities anywhere. It will also respond to liability arising from "insured Locations.""

"Will cover your personal, **_nonbusiness_** activities anywhere." For those of you who think nothing will ever use your liability coverage let me relate a short story.

> *It was the Saturday before Thanksgiving in 1988(the day of the Florida vs. Florida State game and I was hosting a party, Nope, this has nothing to do with the party, but as I was preparing for the party, I got a panicked call from one of my insureds. He was a do-it-yourselfer, after purchasing some boards he was taking them to his car, made a quick turn and hit a man in the head and injured his eye. I called our claims adjuster, and he went directly to the hospital, we paid $186,000.*
> *$100,000 from his homeowner's policy and $86,000 from his umbrella.*

You never know! Purchase as much liability as you can afford.

"It will also respond to liability arising from "insured Locations." Noticed I used the term "RESPOND" one of the most prominent benefits your policy is defense. Remember the cost of defense is over and above your limits.

The term **INSURED LOCATIONS** have an unusually broad definition it includes: the residence premises listed in the Declarations; newly acquired residences during the policy period; locations where an insured is temporarily residing. This would include a hotel room. A location rented for nonbusiness use; this could be a for a wedding reception. Vacant land as long as it is truly vacant land. Many times I would get a call from a prospective insured, they would ask me, "I have 25 acres of land west of 75, will your homeowner's policy cover it?"

I always answer, "as long as it is not used for FARMING (no farming) and it is truly vacant."

They would respond, "Well what about the ten mobile homes I have on it." UGH! – Sorry, no coverage.

A lot of the wording of the policy is vague and refers to your intent. If you are building a home you, INTEND to live in you have liability (NOT PROPERTY) coverage for the site, but if you INTEND to rent out the building, no coverage.

By the way, if someone trips over your great grand father's headstone in a cemetery, check the lineage and sues you, relax your homeowners policy will respond.

I know you want to know what is not covered. Well, this section is designed for the protection of an individual and family. The intent has never been to cover a business exposure, so obviously, business or professional activities are excluded. BUT ! The policy does not exclude any activities which are usual to nonbusiness pursuits.

> *Of course, I will explain. If you are like many of my colleagues, do most of their business on the golf course, and while playing that boring game while swinging at a ball accidentally hits his client and breaks his jaw. Even if, they were discussing business the activity, GOLF, is considered a nonbusiness pursuits and the policy will respond.*

There is some limited business coverage, as an office, or studio has premises coverage. Now I am showing my age, but I remember getting my hair cut at the neighbor's home who had his patio converted into his barber shop. Some companies still may have that endorsement available but, I believe that coverage has become a dinosaur.

The term **INCIDENTAL** strikes fear in the heart of all insurance adjusters; it is like showing a cross to a vampire. If the business activity is deemed **INCIDENTAL,** chances are the policy will respond.

The question which may have to be defined by a court. But, activities for which no insured receives less than $2,000 in compensation per year such as selling fruit and vegetables in your front yard, babysitting and cutting yards with a push mower would fit this category; as well as insured under the age of 21 engaged in a part-time, self-employed business *with no employees.*

Providing childcare services has become problematic. Providing **childcare for no compensation**, and providing childcare services ***for pay for a relative of the insured*** can be covered. Yeah, you got me here. I honestly cannot explain this with confidence. Please understand the definition of **compensation** can be decided by the court.

> *One of my early mentors told me "insurance companies are your best friend as long as the claim is under $5,000. Over $5,000, it becomes real money, and they become cool acquaintances. Recently I read horrific court cases. Summarizing, one lady rented a garage apartment for several years from a family; The renter had a "Renters" policy with a liability limit of $300,000. The renter was laid off temporarily. The family who owned the apartment agreed to waive the rent if the lady would watch their child. All agreed, but while under the renters charge, the child was accidentally scalded.*

The family sued under the renters, renter's policy. The company refused to respond, and the courts upheld. The court rules that the trade, rent for child service was valuable compensation and thereby excluded. --- PLEASE BEWARE!

Let's talk about motorized land vehicles, first, let's look at the definition, A self-propelled wheeled conveyance that does not run on rails. OK, that is very broad and will include automobiles, pickups, vans, trucks, and motorcycles, riding lawnmowers, snow machines, all-terrain vehicles(ATV), golf carts, scooters, go carts. Motorized skateboards. Like I said the definition is very broad so you must understand that the homeowners policy will EXCLUDE coverage for motorized land vehicles. REMEMBER WE ARE TALKING ABOUT LIABILITY.

1. Any vehicles designed to assist the handicapped ***ARE COVERED*** anywhere in the world ***as long as the vehicle is being used to assist a handicapped person at the time of the occurrence***
2. Any motorized land vehicles used solely to service a residence premises ***IS COVERED but only while on your insured location***.
3. Any motor vehicle in ***dead storage*** at the insured location IS ***COVERED*** - The problem is there is not a definition of dead storage in the policy. However, IRMI (http://www.irmi.com) States that dead storage

means the vehicle's electrical system is dead, the battery has been removed, the vehicle is on blocks, or the plates have been removed, and registration turned in.

4. Off-road recreational vehicles are covered while on an insured location if they are **_OWNED_** by an insured, and are covered anywhere in the world if **_NON-OWNED_**.

Let's say you purchase your son a go-cart, and he runs over your neighbor, Mrs. McGillicuddy, if she was on your property, then your Homeowners will respond. If your son is driving his go-cart and runs over Mrs. McGillicuddy on the public street, you **WILL HAVE NO COVERAGE.**

Now here is a twist, if your son is at your brother's house and uses his cousins go cart and runs over Mrs. McGillicuddy in the public street YOUR HOMEOWNERS will respond to pay for her broken hip because Off-road recreational vehicles are covered anywhere in the world if **_NON-OWNED._**

Also, if you go to Ft. Meyers, you can rent these small off-road recreational vehicles that look like Easter Eggs. Because they are **_NON-OWNED_**, you will have coverage under a standard Homeowner policy.

5. The Golf cart. Now here it does get complicated, and I am going to suggest you read your policy and check to see if your state has laws compelling insurance companies to extend coverage from the Homeowners policy. The golf cart, of course, will be

covered on your INSURED LOCATION. There will also be coverage while on a golfing facility, being used for golf. Or other permitted activity. Now here is where it gets particularly tricky, within a private residential community which contains the insured's residence as long as the community has ***authority over the roadways*** in the community and has authorized the use of golf carts on the roads.

BOAT LIABILITY COVERAGE UNDER A HOMEOWNER POLICY.

If there is Liability coverage under the standard insurance policy, the answer is YES. But, honestly, unless all you have is a row boat with less than a 25hp motor, it is not worth mentioning. I would prefer you be safe and assume you have no liability coverage under a homeowners policy.

HOMEOWNERS ENDORSEMENTS

Modifications to the Homeowners Policy are called an endorsement. Here are some endorsements and my comments for each.

- "Inflation Guard" increased your coverage each year.
- If you need additional Coverage B, you may add it by endorsement.,
- Remember the limitations of money and jewelry? You may increase them here: increased: money,

from $200 to $1,000; securities from $1,500 to $2,000; jewelry and furs from $1,500 to $5,000 (subject to $1,000 on any one item); silverware, etc., from $2,500 to $10,000; firearms from $2,500 to $6,500; business property from $2,500 to $10,000; electronic apparatus from $1,500 to $6,000. BUT purchasing a PAF for these items will yield better coverage and a better insurance value.

- Increases losses from credit cards/forgery/counterfeit money may be increased to as much as $10,000. NOTE doing this may cause your policy to be reviewed by underwriting.
- Increase the limit of 10% of Coverage C, which applies to property usually located at a secondary residence or self-storage facility may be increased to any higher amount. For Self-storage facilities, I encourage you to do so. But, for another residence NO! Purchase specific coverage on the additional resident; this could save you problems if there is a claim at the second location.
- Increase property assessment coverage If you have a Homeowners or Condo Association, you may consider an increase. If you DO NOT belong to an HOA, you do not need it.
- Building ordinances or laws coverage is particularly crucial, the older your home, the more you need to purchase.
- REPLACEMENT COST ON PERSONAL PROPERTY IS A MUST!
- In some states, you may be able to endorse a "special coverage" endorsement can be added to the to provide "open peril" coverage to both building property and personal property.
- Some companies offer an assisted living care facility endorsement. This provides coverage for

relatives of an insured in such a long-term care facility. If your parents are in such a long term care facility, this is an excellent idea,

- A newer endorsement allows "CERTAIN" trust eligible for coverage.
- Physical damage coverage for owned golf carts can be added, BUT I contend you are better off purchasing a specific Golf Cart Policy. I DO NOT RECOMMEND THIS ENDORSEMENT.
- Home Business Insurance Coverage endorsements and policies are available. DO NOT ASSUME any of your business operation nor your business personal property EXCEPT for a meager $2,500 is covered. There are many HOME BASED BUSINESS packages that will increase not only your business personal property but can broaden your liability.
- "Personal Injury Liability" adds coverage for claims against the insured for false arrest, detention or imprisonment, malicious prosecution, libel, slander, invasion of privacy, wrongful eviction and wrongful entry. I HIGHLY RECOMMENDED THIS ENDORSEMENT.

DWELLING INSURANCE.

- ✓ So you are a landlord, no you will not be eligible for a homeowners policy unless you are an owner occupant of a duplex, triplex or quadplex. If you do not live in the dwelling, then you must purchase a DWELLING POLICY.

- ✓ Although we did not get into it, Corporations, "BUSINESS" trusts, partnerships, LLC and other 'unnatural persons' cannot have a homeowner's policy and must purchase a dwelling (and in some cases commercial property policies).

If you are a landlord you are a business person, you need this section so get your highlighter out.

Whereas the Homeowner Policies were "Package Policies" that is covering, property and liability and more, the "Dwelling Policies" are usually "Mono-Line" policies; covering only property. You must purchase and/or add Liability through endorsement or another policy. We will discuss that because there are some extremely important things to consider. If you must cover a dwelling, ask your agent if there are any "Landlord Package" policies available. They tend to be very comprehensive in coverage and designed for the small Landlord. If you are in Florida – for-get-about-it, they are not out there so take heed.

Dwelling policies are property policies. Therefore, we are talking about direct payment to you or your lienholder. Remember?

You may also recall I said that there are two parts to property policies a list that lists what will be covered, your Coverages and a list of things that can happen to your stuff, perils.

The Dwelling policy evolved from the 165 line New York Standard Fire Policy written in 1918. Hence, you will hear the Dwelling Policy referred to as a "Fire Policy." Today there are three forms of the modern Dwelling policy, the Basic form *AKA (Also Known As)* the DP1, the Broad form, and the Special Form. Each form has its terms and conditions.

Let's look at the first list – the list of what we will cover.

The Basic Form (DP1)

A – Dwelling

B – Other Structures

C – Personal Property

D – Fair Rental Value

The Broad Form (DP2)

A – Dwelling

B – Other Structures

C – Personal Property

D – Fair Rental Value

E – Additional Living Expenses

The Special Form (DP3)

A – Dwelling

B – Other Structures

C – Personal Property

D – Fair Rental Value

E – Additional Living Expenses

The coverages are remarkably similar to the Coverage definitions in the homeowner policy.

Coverage A – Dwelling - covers the actual dwelling you are renting. And, as in the HO form, it will also include building equipment and outdoor equipment used for the service of BUT located on the premises.

Coverage B - will cover detached structures on the dwelling premises. 10% of coverage A but is not Additional Insurance on the DP 1 but granted as Additional insurance for the DP2 & DP3

Coverage C – Personal Property. This would be for household furnishings owned by the landlord. This is an option, and unless you have very expensive furnishings we usually do not recommend it. (Yes, I will explain)

Coverage D – Your rent, the CASH FLOW you will need to pay the mortgage if there is a loss and becomes uninhabitable from damage by a peril insured against. Remember this is an INDIRECT LOSS! 20% of coverage A but is not Additional Insurance on the DP 1 but granted as <u>Additional insurance</u> for the DP2 & DP3. Remember <u>Additional insurance </u>is paid OVER THER LIMIT of the policy, coverage granted but not additional insurance is paid to the policy limit.

Coverage E – This is for the RARE occasion where you will have an "OWNER OCCUPY" the dwelling. Not available in a DP1 and is granted as Additional insurance for the DP2 & DP3

Trees, Plants, Shrubs are EXCLUDED under the DP1 Basic form but Under a DP2 or a DP3 , is granted as Additional Insurance, 5% of A Coverage but limited to $500, any one tree, plant, or shrub WITH LIMITED PERILS (and one is NOT Wind)

OK, this is your list of what is covered now we will talk about the lists of what perils, things that can happen to your stuff.

There is THREE cause of loss forms, the BASIC, the BROAD, and the SPECIAL form. We talked about this briefly under the homeowner's policy. Now the BASIC for and the BROAD forms are called **NAMED PERIL POLICIES.** Why? Because these forms specifically list what perils are covered, simply if what happens is named on the list (form). The SPECIAL form, like the HO policy, covers everything and lists the exclusion, if what happens to your stuff is not EXCLUDED, it is Covered.

The DP 1, Basic Form is called because we use the Basic List. Here is what it covered:

Fire, lightning, internal explosion. Hopefully, if your agent does recommend a DP1, they should EC or *EXTENDED COVERAGE* which adds the perils of riot or civil commotion, aircraft, vehicles, smoke (excluding smoke from fireplaces, agricultural smudging or industrial operations), and volcanic eruption. If you have added the EC then you may add for an additional premium ***VMM (Vandalism and malicious mischief)***

IMPORTANT

FOR ALL THREE FORMS, VMM is suspended if the dwelling was VACANT for more than 60 DAYS!

Also, to other coverages already mentioned the DP1 will cover the cost of removal of debris after a covered property loss is reimbursed; reasonable costs for necessary repairs to protect the property from further loss, after a covered loss. Coverage is provided, for up to five days, at temporary locations when the property is removed from premises endangered by a peril insured against (BUT coverage will only be granted for the DP1 perils).

Also, the policy will pay up to an additional $500 for fire department service charges of property owners areas which are served by volunteer fire departments who contract with the home owner, to reimburse for fees charged when the FD responds.

DP1 BASIC FORM Loss valuation is on an ACV, Actual Cash Value basis for Coverage A, B, C.

The DP 2, Broad Form is called because we use the Broad List of Covered Perils. Here is what it covered:

First, everything that was in the DP1 (including the EC and VMM) plus:

Damage by burglars, damage done to the actual dwelling while the dwelling is being burgled. Falling objects, any object anyone ever have a "Blue Ice Claim? Weight of ice, snow or sleet which could be significant to northerners (Remember this is NOT included in the DP1) Now this next peril is reason enough NOT to purchase a DP1and that is the ***accidental discharge or overflow of water or steam from within a plumbing, heating, air conditioning or automatic fire protective sprinkler system or from within a household appliance***.

My cousin is a landlord up north and a couple of his properties still have boilers; This peril, ***sudden and accidental tearing apart, cracking, burning or bulging of a steam or hot water heating system, air conditioning system or automatic fire-protective sprinkler system, or water heating appliance***, is also not included in the DP1. So if you go real cheap with the DP1 and your boiler explodes and destroys the rental. NO COVERAGE, you must select at least the DP2.

I think the next peril in the DP2 but not in the DP1 is extremely crucial in all areas or the US. I find that you Northerners understand and know what to do when the temperature drops, but we southerners have no clue so the next peril the ***freezing of plumbing, heating, air conditioning or automatic fire protective sprinkler system or of a household appliance***. Finally, the DP2 Brad form covers the peril of sudden and accidental damage from artificially generated electrical current we know this as power surges.

This should be a no-brainer if you can choose a DP1 or DP2 you must choose at least the DP2 just on the covered perils alone.

You get the additional coverages we mentioned in the DP1 but also 10% of Coverage A which may be applied to other structures (Coverage B) *as additional amounts of insurance*. In addition, to the combination of the rental value and additional living expenses, (if owner occupied) Coverages D and E, the policy will provide 20% of Coverage applying to rental value and if owner occupied and additional living expenses *an additional amount of insurance.*
3. An additional Other Coverage covers loss to trees, shrubs and plants. Five percent of the Coverage A limit may be applied, as an additional amount of insurance, with a limit of $500 on any one tree, shrub or plant, for certain of the perils only. *An additional amount of insurance.*

 I promise I will illustrate *an additional amount of insurance.*

Under the DP2 and DP3 provides thirty days (rather than five days) is the time limit for coverage of property removed from premises endangered by a peril insured against.

Finally, under the DP2 and DP3 the forms provide replacement cost on the dwelling as long as you have insured the dwelling to 80% of the replacement cost at the time of loss.

Example. (Yes, this is a simple illustration to all my adjuster friends)

Insurance Limit is $100,000
The replacement value of your dwelling at the time of loss is $120,000

You have a kitchen fire

The ACV adjustment is $8,000 to repair the damage.
The RCV adjustment is $20,000 to repair the damage.

You will receive the $20,000 to repair the damage.
Why –
Value at the loss - $120,000 x 80% = $96,000. This is your threshold; since you have more than 80% coverage, $100,000, you will be paid the replacement value.

NOTE, contents will be still paid at ACV.

The DP 3, AKA "Special Form" covers the peril unless it is excluded. WHAT? I know Insurance speak!

What is excluded depends on the company so please review the policy. Typical exclusions are termites, insects, vermin, birds as well as loss from enforcement of any law regulating use, construction, demolition or repair of property; earth movement;

water damage from flood, rising waters, backing up of sewers or drains (including water-borne material), overflow from a sump, or subsurface water; damage caused by power interruption if the damaged power source is at other premises; neglect of the insured to protect property from damage; war; nuclear hazards; intentional loss; and governmental action. ***BUT LIKE THE HOMEOWNERS POLICY SPECIAL FORM APPLIES ONLY TO COVERAGE A & B***

Also, there are some additional boarding of coverage under the DP3 the net effect is intended to produce broadened coverage by covering miscellaneous, undefined incidents. For example, under the DP 1 and DP2, you would have to show damage to the building before interior damage will be covered whereas the DP3 will cover water damage from the water being forced under shingles and damage from that contingency where this would not be covered under the DP1 or DP2. Also to the DP3 theft of property that is an integral part of the dwelling such as the Air Conditioner. Whereas under the DP1 – DP2 there would be no coverage.

Final thoughts about the dwelling program, your choices should be the DP2 or DP3. You may recall I said I did not recommend covering Landlord furnishings. The valuation is going to be ACV Actual Cash Value, which means the furnishing will be depreciated, and furnishings depreciate much faster than the dwelling itself. Secondly, you will have furniture broken, and a lot of times the furnishings will disappear. Neither are covered perils. I think your risk management should be "Taking deposits" to cover both cleaning and loss of furnishings and should not be insured.

Landlord Liability.

First, you do not have enough. You want to make sure you purchase Liability coverage to cover any occurrences that happen on your rented premises. You should consider least $1,000,000 of coverage. YOU ARE RESPONSIBLE for what happens on YOUR property, and unless you live next door, you can not know what is happening on your property.

PERSONAL INJURY!

When you shop for coverage make sure your Liability Coverage includes ***PERSONAL INJURY,*** which is one of the misunderstood coverage by even most insurance agents. ***PERSONAL INJURY*** covers claims against the insured for false arrest, detention or imprisonment, malicious prosecution; wrongful entry or eviction; and oral or written publications that libel, slander, or violation of rights of private occupancy.

As you can see unless you have this coverage, you could have no coverage for wrongful entry, wrongful eviction, or an invasion of privacy. All who are exposures you as a landlord have. Insist on this coverage.

USE AN ATTORNEY!

It may cost a few hundred dollars to have one but well worth it. In your interview talk about requiring the tenants to secure renters coverage, as well as holding you harmless for dogs, animals, and illegal act. Your attorney will understand and draft a least to protect you if your insurance cannot.

Umbrella – Excess Liability

The philosophy of our agency is to retain as much property exposure as you can and purchase as much liability coverage as you can afford. We recommend that everyone who owns a home or has money in savings purchase an ***UMBRELLA POLICY***.

All Umbrella Policies are Excess Liability Policies, but not all Excess Liability Policies ARE NOT ***UMBRELLA POLICIES.***

So you are asking, what is the difference An excess liability policy only extends the individual policies over their limits for an excess amount you select. For example, if you own a home, and an auto you purchase coverage over and above the coverage you already have; you have split limits of $100,000/$300,000/$100,000 and purchase an ***EXCESS LIABILITY*** policy of $1,000,000 then if you are sued you have an extra $1,000,000 coverage. BUT an ***EXCESS LIABILITY*** will only add coverage to policies you already have. If you rent a boat and have an accident, your ***EXCESS LIABILITY*** will be useless and WILL NOT RESPOND!

An ***UMBRELLA POLICY,*** on the other hand, has two features that identify it as a *TRUE **UMBRELLA POLICY**.* The features are a DROP DOWN and a SIR (Self Insured

Retention). Now using the same scenario you rented a boat and had an accident now a true ***UMBRELLA POLICY*** will "DROP DOWN" to the SIR, which for the most part is a deductible and will respond.

Just like if you open an umbrella and try to set it down the umbrella will fall without someone with fingers to hold it. An insurance ***UMBRELLA POLICY*** works the same way you must hold an UMBRELLA with fingers of coverage. If you own an auto policy, generally you must have liability insurance of at least $250,000/$500,000/$100.000 (there are some umbrellas will allow $100,000/$300,000/$100,00 with a surcharge). If you own a home, you must have at least $300,000 of Liability for your home if you own rental property you must have $300,000 on each property, and if you own watercraft, you must cover the watercraft at $300,000. As long as you keep your under laying coverage in force any incident that is not covered the policy will respond.

The price difference between an ***EXCESS POLICY*** and a ***UMBRELLA POLICY*** is minimal, and we make every effort to convince our clients to purchase a true ***UMBRELLA POLICY.*** A word of caution there are websites that tout themselves as selling ***UMBRELLA POLICIES*** but are ***EXCESS POLICIES*** be careful.

HIGH PROFILE PERSONALITIES AND PROPERTIES

Just a special note, even if you are the weather guy or gal in a small television market, please spend a couple of hours talking with a licensed insurance agent. You are a target and need protection from frivolous lawsuits.

PERSONAL INLAND MARINE POLICIES

A/K/A - PERSONAL ARTICLES FLOATERS (PAF)

You now should have two questions; what is a *PERSONAL INLAND MARINE POLICY*? And the more urgent question is why do I need one?

Let's say you are going on a cruise and you purchase a $3,500 camera to take pictures on the trip. While you are pulling out of port, you decide to lean over your balcony rail to take some brilliant shots. When you stand, the lariat breaks and your camera falls into the ocean.

Well, all you have to do is call the bridge and ask the Captain to stop the ship and go back to and retrieve your camera. Good luck with that, you may even get laughed at. Now the question I have for you is this incident covered under your homeowner's policy?

First you need to recall that under the standard HO3 your personal property is subject to the "Named Peril" "Broad Form" cause of loss form which are:

> *Fire; lightning; windstorm; hail; explosion; riot or civil commotion; aircraft; vehicles; smoke; vandalism or malicious mischief;*

theft; falling objects; weight of ice, snow or sleet; accidental discharge or overflow of water or steam from within a plumbing, heating, air conditioning or sprinkler system or household appliance; sudden and accidental tearing apart, cracking, burning or bulging of a steam or hot water heating, air conditioning or sprinkler system or water heating appliance; freezing of a plumbing, heating, air conditioning, sprinkler system or household appliance; sudden and accidental damage from artificially generated electrical current; volcanic eruption.

Unfortunately, stupidity, not checking the strap or the strap breaking is not on the list above so you would have no coverage but READ ON!

One of the characteristics of anything covered under a **_PERSONAL INLAND MARINE POLICY (PAF)_** is *"portability."* So with that being said, we are talking about now- professional; Cameras, Musical Instruments, Fine Arts, Stamp and Coin Collections, Golfer's Equipment, Silverware, Jewelry, and Furs.

✓ As you remember when we discussed your homeowner's policy we pointed out that there are limitations to certain property for the theft of as jewelry, silverware, furs and more. The PAF also expands the perils insured against. The perils are as close to "ALL RISKS" as you can get, the standard PAF covers all perils except for wear and tear, deterioration, inherent vice, government action, and loss caused by insects or vermin.

Now let's revisit the loss of your camera on your cruise. If you would have called your agent and added a PAF to cover your camera, now you *WOULD* have coverage because stupidity, not checking the strap or the strap breaking is NOT EXCLUDED under the PAF and, therefore, covered.

Generally, PAF's have no deductible, and if the PAF is available under your homeowners policy the coverage is remarkably inexpensive, and coverage is worldwide. There are some considerations you must understand. The term ***INHERENT VICE***. An ***INHERENT VICE*** is a hidden defect (or the very nature) of a physical object that causes it to deteriorate because of the fundamental instability of the components of which it is made.

Story: in 1988, I had an insured who had over $150,000 in Jewelry covered under a PAF. He called and explained that when he retrieved his wife's diamond ring from the safe, he noticed it was "cracked" inside the ring. A "flaw" within the diamond fractured rendering the ring worthless. We denied coverage, but the good news is on the appraisal we noted the seller gave a warranty against ***INHERENT VICE.*** The jeweler gladly replaced the diamond.

HINT: When purchasing jewelry always ask if the seller will warrant the jewels for ***INHERENT VICE.***

Other PAF issues you need to know about. I only know of two companies who will give replacement cost or "AGREED VALUE" on PAF items, most companies will pay for the LESSER of ACV; cost to repair or replace. The problem you are paying for a dollar amount says you are paying the premium for a $10,000 ring. The ring is lost; the company can replace or "replicate" the ring for $5,000, and the ACV is $6,500, you will get the new ring.

To have a PAF written for an item, you will need a current (within two years) appraisals for most classes under a PAF. Once you have committed to the PAF, you must make sure you keep your appraisals up to date.

EXAMPLE

An insured gets a pair of gold earrings for the value at the time of purchase $10,000 and orders a PAF from their agent for $10,000. Six months later one earring is lost. The company will pay the difference between the policy limit, less what the value of the REMAINING earring which just after Six months would be about $5,000.

If you DO NOT update your appraisal, and after five years you lose one earring, and the value of the pair is now $15,000, the value of the remaining earring is $7,500 you will only receive $2,500 for the loss. That is $10,000 (Policy Limit as you DID NOT update your appraisal), less the value of the remaining earrings, $7,500.

Whatever you add to a PAF, you must keep up your appraisals.

Standard carriers will let you and Cameras, Musical Instruments, Fine Arts, Stamp and Coin Collections, Golfer's Equipment, Silverware, Jewelry, and Furs. There are a few companies who will insure your guns. We recommend your join the NRA and take advantage of their insurance programs.

DIFFERENT RULES FOR FINE ARTS

FINE ARTS is a valued policy; that is the claims value valuation "will pay for the LESSER of ACV; the cost to repair or replace" does not apply. Under fine arts, the insured value IS THE VALUE the company will pay in case of loss. Since all "FINE ART" is considered "ONE OF A KIND"; the company does not have the option to replace, they must pay the face amount of the policy.

There is also a difference in which a "Pair or Set" is adjusted. Let's say that you have a pair of bronze sculptures that are intertwined. The value of the Pair is $50,000, and you have insured the Pair under a PAF. There is a house fire, and you were only able to save one of the sets, the other was destroyed. The company will give you the face amount of the policy

BUT YOU MUST SURRENDER the undamaged part of the set.

One word of caution does not be generous with your art. It is true you have "World Wide" coverage, but if you allow your art to be on public display or exhibition, your "PERSONAL" Article Floater will NOT RESPOND.

If you allow your art to be on display, make sure there is a "Commercial" Fine Arts policy in force that names not only the art but you as owner and insured.

Appraisals must be updated at least every two years

Flood Insurance

✓ *First of all, we really want to make sure you understand what a flood is. It is not a pipe breaking. That would be "Water Damaged" and covered under the homeowners policy.*

✓ *According to the NFIP Flood, as used in this flood insurance policy means:*

     ○ *A general and temporary condition of partial or complete inundation of two or more acres of normally dry land area or two or more properties (at least one of which is your property) from:*

          ■ *a. Overflow of inland or tidal waters;*

          ■ *b. Unusual and rapid accumulation of runoff of surface waters from any source;*

          ■ *c. Mudflow*

     ○ *Collapse or subsidence of land along the shore of a lake or similar body of water as a result of erosion or undermining caused by waves or currents of water exceeding anticipated cyclical levels that result in a flood as defined above.*

✓ *Flood is caused by "Raising waters" from a body of water. The key point is there must be inundation to both your property AND your neighbors or if you have no neighbor the inundation must be at least two acres*

If you live in Florida or live within ten miles of a body of water, you should purchase a flood policy! If your community is enrolled in the ***NATIONAL FLOOD INSURANCE PROGRAM (NFIP)*** your property is in a flood zone.

Here are the zones definitions by the NFIP:

Zones B, C, and X: These areas have been identified in the community flood insurance study as areas of moderate or minimal hazard from the principal source of flood in the area. However, buildings in these zones could be flooded by severe, concentrated rainfall coupled with inadequate local drainage systems. Local storm water drainage systems are not normally considered in the community's Flood Insurance Study. The failure of a local drainage system creates areas of high flood risk within these rate zones. Flood insurance is available in participating communities but is not required by regulation in these zones. (Zone X is used on new and some revised maps in place of Zones B and C.)

A Zones - Areas subject to inundation by the 1-percent-annual-chance flood event determined using approximate methodologies. Because detailed hydraulic analyzes have not been performed, no Base Flood Elevations (BFEs) or flood depths are shown. Mandatory flood insurance purchase requirements and floodplain management standards apply.

Zone AE and A1-30 - Areas subject to inundation by the 1-percent-annual-chance flood event determined by detailed methods. Base Flood Elevations (BFEs) are shown. Mandatory flood insurance purchase requirements and floodplain management standards apply.

Zone AH - Areas subject to inundation by 1-percent-annual-chance shallow flooding (usually areas of ponding) where average depths are between one and three feet. Base Flood Elevations (BFEs) derived from detailed hydraulic analyzes are shown in this zone. Mandatory flood insurance purchase requirements and floodplain management standards apply

Zone AO - Areas subject to inundation by 1-percent-annual-chance shallow flooding (usually sheet flow on sloping terrain) where average depths are between one and three feet. Average flood depths derived from detailed hydraulic analyzes are shown in this zone. Mandatory flood insurance purchase requirements and floodplain management standards apply. Some Zone AO are designated in areas with high flood velocities such as alluvial fans and washes. Communities are encouraged to adopt more restrictive requirements for these areas.

Zone AR - Areas that result from the decertification of a previously accredited flood protection system that is determined to be in the process of being restored to provide base flood protection. Mandatory flood insurance purchase requirements and floodplain management standards apply.

Zone A99 - Areas subject to inundation by the 1-percent-annual-chance flood event, but which will ultimately be protected upon completion of an under-construction Federal flood protection system. These are areas of special flood hazard where enough progress has been made on the construction of a protection system, such as dikes, dams, and levees, to consider it complete for insurance rating purposes. Zone A99 may only be used when the flood protection system has reached specified statutory progress toward completion. No Base Flood Elevations (BFEs) or depths are shown. Mandatory flood insurance purchase requirements and floodplain management standards apply.

Zone V - Areas along coasts subject to inundation by the 1-percent-annual-chance flood event with additional hazards associated with storm-induced waves. Because detailed hydraulic analyzes have not been performed, no Base Flood Elevations (BFEs) or flood depths are shown. Mandatory flood insurance purchase requirements and floodplain management standards apply.

Zone VE and V1-30 - Areas subject to inundation by the 1-percent-annual-chance flood event with additional hazards due to storm-induced velocity wave action. Mandatory flood insurance purchase requirements and floodplain management standards apply.

For more information go to www.floodsmart.gov

I know your eyes are glazing over now, but, here is what you need to know. Since most federal agencies are incestuous if you apply for a "Federally Insured Loan" it will be mandatory for you to purchase flood coverage for the life of the loan if you are in any zone that is an A or V zone.

The B C or X Zones are known as "Preferred Flood Zones" and afford coverage at very affordable prices.

Any agent who sells flood coverage should be able to run a "Flood Zone Determination" AT NO COST TO YOU!

If you are in a B C or X Zone, the agent can give you a cost of flood insurance easily. If you are in any other zone, you must determine if your home is "PRE-FIRM" or "POST-FIRM.

If your home or business is in the floodplain and was constructed before 12/31/1974, it is considered to be Pre-FIRM. Pre-FIRM means it was constructed before identification of the FIRM while Post-FIRM means it was constructed after this date. If your property is Pre-FIRM no elevation certificate will be needed to establish a rate., However, if, you property Post-FIRM constructed AFTER 12/31/1974 an elevation certificate MUST BE SENT TO THE AGENT TO ESTABLISH A RATE!

Property in any "V" zone presents other issues. "V" indicates you are in a velocity zone this also may be referred to as a "Wave Wash Area." If you apply for a property insurance policy that includes wind many companies will insist you purchase and maintain a flood policy to have wind coverage. Why? Excellent questions. We just went through "Super Storm Sandy" and all of us have seen the damage. Many of the homes were in or near wave wash areas and only had wind coverage. But, who can tell if the damage was because of "Wind Driven Rain," covered by the wind policy or was the damage done by the force of rising water, covered by flood. If you had both policies in force, you would have coverage, either from the wind coverage or flood. Unfortunately, we are finding that most of the losses the insureds only had wind coverage.

The flood policy is essential because the only place you can get a flood policy is through the NFIP. All flood policies are rated the same way and all rates for the same coverage, and the same deductibles should be IDENTICAL. Many companies will affix their name to the front page of the policy, but the next pages will be the standard NFIP policy.

The policy is lacking in a very valuable coverage; that is a loss or rental income or additional living expenses. So if, the cause of your loss is flood your property will be repaired, but you will have to pay your own expenses while the repairs are being made.

The flood policy had an 80 – 80 rule that is in order to be paid replacement cost you must live in the property 80% of the time and insured to 80% to value. If you rent the property to others, your loss will be adjusted on an ACV basis; that is the cost to repair or replace less depreciation.

NEW Information non primary resident policies will be assessed and additional $250 per year. As of this writing the flood rules have changed, yet again. Please check our website for updates.

Personal Property will be adjusted on an ACV basis.

The flood policy also limits the base coverage to $250,000 for residential buildings and $500,000 for nonresidential. This brings up the need for excess flood coverage which is written by companies other than NFIP. We highly recommend you purchase excess coverage.

FLOOD RECOMMENDATIONS.

Purchase as much dwelling coverage as you require, usually the maximum amount.

Purchase the MAXIMUM deductible as you can or your mortgage company will let you.

Consider self-insuring personal property, remember it will be adjusted on an ACV basis.

Always purchase coverage if your property is in a "V" Zone.

Purchase excess flood coverage if the value is above the maximum offered by the flood policy.

If you are an investor and holding the property for rent, if you have no mortgage or the property is in a BC or X zone you need to consider self-insurance if the property is more than 25 years old and you have not made substantial improvement. However, if your property is in a "V" Zone, purchase flood because of the wave wash rule.

Insuring your Toys

We are talking about Recreational Vehicles, Motorcycles, Off-Road Vehicles, Antique Autos, Boats, and Personal Watercraft, electronics.

Recreational Vehicles are defined as any vehicle that has a kitchen, a bathroom, a bedroom or sleeping area and is self-propelled. If the vehicles are designed to be pulled by an auto or truck. Then the vehicle is endorsed on to your personal auto policy, but if it is self-propelled, then you must purchase a separate policy if your personal auto carrier does not offer a "Miscellaneous Auto Endorsement."

Recreational Vehicles

The cost of Recreational Vehicles can range from $10,000 to over $1,000,000. Obviously, you must cover liability, medical as well as uninsured and under- insured motorist in addition to physical damage. There are other coverages you should consider:

- Roadside assistance.
- The Emergency Assistance Package includes Transportation, meals, and lodging.
- Audio, visual, and customized equipment.

If you loan or lease the RV, you must notify your carrier and add a "Loan/Lease Endorsement.",

Motorcycles – In addition to the coverages under an auto policy, it is vital that you must endorse coverage to protect any passengers riding with you. Remember to cover any custom equipment. Some companies may even offer coverage for safety apparel.

Off-road vehicles, Liability coverage, is a must including passenger liability. There are options for medical payments and physical damage to cover the vehicle itself.

Antique Cars. Antique cars are treated the same as other cars with a few exceptions.

The Value must be backed up by an appraisal from a qualified appraiser within two years. The car must be at least 25 years old or be considered a "Modern Classic."

The age of what cars a company will take under different programs is "Company Specific."

A word of caution, most Antique/Collector policies have a mileage cap and is shown on the Dec page . It is prudent to log every mile and keep your agent informed should you are close to the mileage cap.

One thing I want to point out, the value stated and insured is not necessarily what will be paid if there is a loss only the starting point to determine the ACV.

Boats and Watercraft. First, do not assume you have any coverage for a boat under your home owners policy, it is either limited or nonexistent. There is no standard boat policy. Each company in each state tweaks their policies, then file the policy form with the state to meet the needs of boat owners in that state.

1. Liability! I cannot stress this enough, we live in a highly litigious society, and you need to protect your assets. Just because, the boat is small, don't for the second think that you cannot have a liability loss. In 30 years in this business, I have seen some truly strange claims. At a minimum for small boats $300,000 of liability.
    a. Larger boats (28 – 50 feet): - $500,000 and don't forget to add it to your umbrella.
    b. Cigarette Boats: and other power boats. $1,000,000 with an umbrella. Why? The fact you own such a boat makes you a "RICH" target for a litigator.
    c. Personal Watercraft: Most get in trouble not owning one but when they impulsively rent one on vacation. Let me make this abundantly clear. YOU HAVE NO LIABILITY COVERAGE UNDER YOUR HOMEOWNERS POLICY. If you own a Personal watercraft, there are policies that reasonably priced, and many will

endorse a non-owned coverage in case you rent one while on vacation.

I hate to be the bearer of bad news, but now you know! In Florida, we have had enormous "uncovered" liability claims because of the EXCLUSION under the homeowners policy. There are a few personal umbrella policies that will respond. When you are purchasing coverage, this is a question you must ask your agent. If your agent tells you, you have coverage under you homeowners immediately follow up with an email with a CC to yourself!

2. Medical Payments works the same way auto medical payments do; $1,000 up is available, our recommendation $1,000 with high limits of liability will be sufficient.

3. Physical Damage to your boat. There are a few companies who will offer "Replacement Cost for the hull, but most companies provide coverage on an agreed value basis for total losses of the hull. Look for policies that will cover other equipment, including motors, unattached equipment, permanently attached equipment, tenders, dinghies inclusively under one dollar amount. If you own a trailer, make sure you ask if theft is covered without exception or exclusion.,

4. As everyone becomes more and more environmentally conscience, you must make sure the policy you purchase will cover Fuel spill and wreckage removal. If it does not,

purchase the endorsement. If an endorsement is not available,purchase with extreme caution

5. If you are having problems with your car, chances are there will be someone who can come to assist you or at the worst walk for help. Not so on the water towing and assistance is critical and purchasing a towing and assistance coverage is a must.

It's about more than the boat

- Some companies will even insure Personal Effects which covers fishing gear and other personal property and other Unattached Equipment automatically such as water-skis, safety equipment, and marine electronics.

Remember you must ask questions when making this purchase.

Considerations – Recommendations

I know that most of you are now purchasing your insurance coverage over the internet. Granted you will save about 10% to 15% on your premiums purchased online. The reason you save is simple, there is no agent to guide you, and if you believe you do not need an agent, and you can keep up on coverages, then you need to continue to purchase your coverage online.

But, if you are not sure or you have significant assets to protect I highly recommend you purchase through an insurance agent. Our agency, Nusurance ® gives you both, the convenience purchasing online but yet you will still have an agent assigned to you to know you and your needs.

If I got you thinking, let me ask you one other question? When you purchased direct from the carrier, do you think that the person you are dealing with on the phone or online will ever speak to you again? Chances are, no. The person on the phone selling you a policy has no vested interested in keeping you a client whereas an independent agent needs you and wants to keep you.

The fact is you will never talk to that person again, and they need to do one thing that is "close you." Make you buy the policy if it does not fit the do not care. If you have an agent, they have a responsibility to explain and more important recommend coverage.

Remember, always check the coverage you purchase with your current coverage. If your new coverage is less than what had you need to know why? A few years ago I lost a client to a phone solicitation from a direct national carrier. The client called to tell me he saved $100 per year and a $100 was $100. I volunteered to review his policy, but he assured me the sales person on the phone guaranteed the coverage was identical.

Eight months later I received a call from an attorney it seems my ex-clients' wife was in a horrible car accident and was now a quadriplegic. I had made sure while the client was my insured he had $300,000 of an uninsured motorist, the new company $10,000. Our agency sent the attorney copies of the EX-insureds showing the coverage. Please beware, the person on the phone will never talk with you again, will never see you, and certainly does not care. They are trained to close the policy, don't "over" explain, sell the policy.

I love to talk insurance. When I meet a new client in my office or via video conference the first thing I ask them is; "What is important to you?" Some will tell me they just want to make it to tomorrow; others are concerned with being sued if their teenager is in an accident.

Here are some Suggestions (Remember to council with your agent):

   1. Young and on your own, little assets and single. Auto Insurance - Liability a step above the state minimum.
Uninsured/Underinsured motorist equal to your liability
Medical Payments
Physical damage with a low deductible with rental reimbursement.

If you are just getting started in life, you need to understand the responsibility and need to purchase liability coverage, at least, one level above the state minimum. You need to cover your injuries with uninsured motorist coverage in case you are injured by someone who has no insurance. Medical Payments; a must if you have no health coverage.

I recommend no matter how old your car is if you are just getting started you need to protect the car as you most likely will not have the assets to replace the auto without help.

Renters; it is very cheap coverage, and if you are just getting started, accumulating assets, you need to protect them, buy the coverage.

2. Young married, renter, little assets
Auto Insurance - Liability a step above the state minimum.
Uninsured/Underinsured motorist equal to your liability
Medical Payments

Physical damage with a low deductible with rental reimbursement.

Renters; it is very cheap coverage, and if you are just getting started, accumulating assets, you need to protect them, buy the coverage

3. Young married, purchase of new home:
Auto Insurance - Liability $100,000/$300,000. Or CSL of $300,000
Uninsured/Underinsured motorist equal to your liability.
Medical Payments.
Physical damage with a low deductible with rental reimbursement.
Homeowners Coverage.
PAF on Wedding Rings.

4. Middle age with or without children Homeowner:
Auto Insurance - Liability $250,000 /$500,000. Or CSL of $500,000
Uninsured/Underinsured motorist equal to your liability.
Medical Payments.
Physical damage with a high deductible and at this point consider self-insurance of cars ten years or older; a rental reimbursement is an option.
Umbrella Policy
Homeowners Coverage.
PAF on Wedding Rings and any other accumulated asset that will fall under an eligible class.

5. Middle age with or without children NON Homeowner (No significant savings):

Auto Insurance - Liability $100,000/$300,000. Or CSL of $300,000
Uninsured/Underinsured motorist equal to your liability.
Medical Payments.
Physical damage with a high deductible and at this point consider self-insurance of cars ten years or older; rental reimbursement is an option.
Umbrella Policy a must consideration
Renters.
PAF on Wedding Rings and any other accumulated asset that will fall under an eligible class.

6. Retired NON Homeowner (No significant savings except IRA / Pension):

Auto Insurance - Liability $100,000/$300,000. Or CSL of $300,000

Uninsured/Underinsured motorist; at this point, you need to make other considerations. If you have a long care policy, and you do not have guest passengers, you can consider a lower if not the minimal limit of coverage. *Uninsured/Underinsured motorist becomes less important as a person becomes older and the awards from Uninsured/Underinsured motorist claims tend to be lower.* Medical Payments.

Physical damage with a high deductible and at this point consider self-insurance of cars ten years or older; rental reimbursement is an option.

Umbrella Policy a must consideration

Renters.

PAF on Wedding Rings and any other accumulated asset that will fall under an eligible class

7. Retired Homeowner (Significant savings):

Auto Insurance - Liability $250,000 /$500,000. Or CSL of $500,000

Uninsured/Underinsured motorist; at this point, you need to make other considerations. If you have a long care policy, and you do not have guest passengers, you can consider a lower if not the minimal limit of coverage. *Uninsured/Underinsured motorist becomes less important as a person becomes older and the awards from Uninsured/Underinsured motorist claims tend to be lower.* Medical Payments.

Physical damage with a high deductible and at this point consider self-insurance of cars ten years or older; rental reimbursement is an option.

Umbrella Policy at least over your aggregate assets.

Homeowners.

PAF on Wedding Rings and any other accumulated asset that will fall under an eligible class.

PLEASE REMEMBER TO COUNCIL WITH YOUR PERSONAL AGENT TO CUSTOMIZE AN INSURANCE PLAN.

Information on understanding your insurance policy.

Insurance Speak

Actual Cash Value (ACV) – The cost to replace an item of property at the time of loss, less an allowance for depreciation. Often used to determine the amount of reimbursement for a loss (Replacement Cost - Depreciation).
At the time of adjustment the adjuster will deduct value because of the item's age. Should you have a large loss not purchasing the Replacement Cost Endorsement could be devastation, always purchase the Replacement cost endorsement.

Admitted Insurance Companies - Companies who register their rate tables with the State. Any premium increases or reductions must be approved by the state before they can be put to market. Admitted carriers are monitored and regulated by their respective state. (See Non-Admitted) You should always consider purchasing from an Admitted carrier over a "Non-Admitted." In most states, Admitted Carriers provide better coverage and conditions than "Non-Admitter" Carriers.

All Risk Insurance – FIRST there is no such thing! A better term would be "open perils" or "Special form", it is insurance protecting the insured from loss arising from any peril other than those perils specifically excluded by name. This contrasts with Named Peril insurance, which names the peril or perils insured against. See Named Peril.

A.M. Best Company provides news, credit **ratings** and financial data products and services for the insurance industry. In Florida, many carriers are NOT AM BEST Rated. Florida uses "Demotech" to rate carriers.

Blanket Insurance – Insurance where a single amount of insurance applies to two or more coverage items. See Specific insurance. Mostly used in Commercial insurance.

Bodily Injury – Usually defined to include physical harm, sickness, disease, or death resulting from any of these.

Casualty Insurance – A line of insurance which historically has included a wide variety of unrelated coverages other than Life and Health. One important coverage in the casualty line is Liability.

Causes of Loss Form – A form which is a part of the Commercial Property Coverage Part of the Commercial Package Policy. It specifies what perils are insured against and lists exclusions. Several different versions provide increasingly broad coverage from Basic to Broad to Special. An earthquake form is also available.

Claim – The assertion of a legal right against an insurer that carries with it a demand for appropriate relief.

Coinsurance Clause – A clause that requires an insured to pay part of a loss if the coverage provided under the policy limits is less than a specified percentage of the value of the property at the time of loss.

Condominium Association Coverage Form – AKA – The Condo Master Policy, a Commercial Package Policy, which covers the buildings in a condominium complex (not the unit owner's personal property). **See FL Law!**

Contingent Liability – Liability which an insured or business incurs because of the actions of others (i.e.,family or employees). Also called vicarious liability.

Contract – A legal agreement between two parties promising a certain performance in exchange for a certain consideration. An Insurance Contract is a contract of adhesion; that is it is not bargained or negotiated. The insured takes the policy as written by the insurance company.

Coverage Trigger – The event which triggers coverage under a Commercial General Liability Coverage form. Under the Occurrence form, the coverage trigger is bodily injury or property damage which occurs during the policy period, regardless of any later time at which a claim is made. Under the Claims-Made form, the trigger is BI or PD which occurs on or after the retroactive date and for which claim is made during the policy period.

Debris Removal – A coverage provided in many property contracts which reimburses the insured for expenses
involved in removing debris produced by a loss from a peril insured against.

Declarations – Usually the first section of an insurance contract that gives the rest of the contract life. It shows who is insured, what property or risk is covered, when and where coverage is effective and how much coverage applies.

Deductible – Usually, a dollar amount the insured must pay on each loss to which the deductible applies. The insurance company pays the remainder of each covered loss up to the policy limits.

Demotech, Inc. has provided responsive services to address actuarial and financial analysis issues, for Florida Insurance Companies.

Direct Loss – Loss which is a direct result of a peril. Also includes loss due to efforts to end the peril or to unavoidable exposure following a peril.

Fidelity Bond – A class of bonds which guarantees an employee's honesty. Today this coverage is provided through Employee Dishonesty insurance.

Fiduciary – A person or institution which has responsibility for the money, property or financial affairs of another.

Flood - A general and temporary condition of partial or complete inundation of two or more acres of normally dry
land area or two or more properties (at least one of which is your property) from: a. Overflow of inland or tidal waters; b. Unusual and rapid accumulation of runoff of surface waters from any source; c. Mudflow

Full Coverage – There is no such thing! Please do not use this term. Many use this term to indicate they want liability as well as physical damage for auto insurance. The problem is what level of coverage is desired. Please take the time to talk with your agent.

Indirect Loss – An Economic loss which is a result or consequence of a direct loss. Loss of rent is an indirect loss.

Inflation Guard – A property insurance option which provides that the policy limits will increase a certain percentage at regular intervals, for instance, annually.

Insurable Interest – Any actual, lawful and substantial economic interest in the safety or preservation of the subject of the insurance free from loss, destruction or pecuniary damage or impairment. A claim may be paid only when an insurable interest exists at TIME OF LOSS for Property and Casualty Policies. (NOTE Life insurance is different)

Insurance – A contract whereby one undertakes to indemnify another or pay or allow a specified amount or a determinable benefit upon determinable contingencies.

Insurance Service Office (ISO) – An organization made up of member companies, which collects and analyzes statistics collected from members and then establishes and files standard rates for many lines of insurance. Also develops standardized forms.

Legal Liability – Rules of law dictate that a person must pay for damages done to another.

Negligence – The failure to exercise that degree of care that the law requires to protect others from an unreasonable risk of harm. The failure to act as a prudent person would have acted under similar circumstances.

Non-Admitted companies Also known as Excess & Surplus Companies are NOT monitored and regulated by the state in which they are Licensed to do business in. They not bound by the same laws as an Admitted Companies. Policy Forms, and Rates are NOT regulated and approved by the state regulators.

Obligee – In bonds, the one who is to be guaranteed that the principal will perform.

Occurrence – In Liability policies, generally defined to be an accident, including continuous or repeated Exposure to substantially the same general harmful conditions.

Occurrence Form – A Commercial General Liability Coverage form with a coverage trigger that states that coverage applies only to bodily injury or property damage which occur during the policy period, regardless of when claim is made.

Ordinance or Law Coverage - Provides to demolish and/or remove and undamaged portion of the existing building to conform with local ordinance and/or pays for increased expenses of building to confirm with current building laws.

Personal Injury – Coverage provided under Liability policies which provides coverage against liability for libel, slander, violation of privacy.

Proximate Cause – A fundamental doctrine in property insurance that holds that when there is an unbroken connection between an occurrence and damage that grows out of the occurrence, then the resulting damage is a part of the occurrence.

CLUE (**Comprehensive Loss Underwriting Exchange**) **CLUE** is a claims-information **report** generated by LexisNexis®, a consumer-**reporting** agency.

Replacement Cost – The cost to replace a damaged or destroyed item of property, without deducting depreciation. May be the basis of reimbursement for loss to buildings, or by endorsement, to personal property.

Replacement Cost Endorsement – An endorsement that can be added to an HO-3 form to provide replacement cost coverage on personal property (with limitations). SEE ACV

Straight Deductible – A deductible that specifies the deduction of a flat amount from a loss payment, regardless of the size of the loss.

Subrogation – The transfer to the insurance company of the insured's right to collect for damages. If you are NOT AT FAULT in an accident and you are not able to contact the other drivers carrier, you look to your carrier to pay for damages to your auto. In this care you pay the deductible. Once you endorse the check you give the company to go under you to recover the damages from the AT FAULT driver and/or their carrier. When the company recovers a percentage you will recover that exact percentage of your deductible.

Vandalism And Malicious Mischief (VMM) – Protects property against damage caused by vandals. Many property forms contain Vandalism and Malicious Mischief coverage.

Vicarious Liability – Negligence which is not directly attributable to the person claimed against, but which is the negligence of another for whom the person claimed against is in some way responsible. See Contingent Liability.

Book 71716CPK

www.ingramcontent.com/pod-product-compliance
Lightning Source LLC
Chambersburg PA
CBHW072202280526
45788CB00002B/839